LANDMARK COLLECTOR'S LIBRARY

Treasures of York

Christine Kyriacou, Frances Mee and Nicola Rogers

Y·O·R·K

ARCHAEOLOGICAL

T·R·U·S·T

Cromwell House, 13 Ogleforth,
York YO1 7FG England
Tel: (01904) 663000 Fax: (01904) 663024
e-mail: enqiries@yorkarchaeology.co.uk
web site: www.yorkarchaeology.co.uk

York Archaeological Trust was created in 1972 in response to the threats posed to the city's archaeological heritage by the redevelopment taking place at that time. Between 1972 and 2003 the Trust carried out over 1,250 archaeological investigations in York, including nearly 200 full-scale excavations and over 1,000 observations during construction or demolition work.

The Trust employs a team of highly skilled people who excavate and record, conserve and curate, research and analyse, publish and exhibit. Our collection of artefacts, a small number of which are illustrated and discussed in this book, is especially important. Many objects which don't normally survive — such as those made of cloth, wood and leather — have been protected by the special soil conditions in some parts of York. This material evidence has allowed us to piece together a picture of the city's past inhabitants.

The Trust is an independent charity and its prime objective is to educate the public in archaeology. To this end, between 1972 and 2003 it has introduced over 13,000,000 visitors to archaeology through the Jorvik Viking Centre and 560,000 visitors through the Archaeological Resource Centre. The results of all the excavation, research, analysis and interpretation undertaken by members of the Trust are available through publications in the 20-volume printed series *The Archaeology of York*, the new *Archaeology of York web series* and the *Yorkshire Archaeology Today* magazine. The archive of records and finds is available to the public and scholars alike.

You could support our work, and keep up to date with our findings, by becoming a Friend of York Archaeological Trust.

LANDMARK COLLECTOR'S LIBRARY

Treasures of York

Christine Kyriacou, Frances Mee and Nicola Rogers

Landmark Publishing

Published by

Ashbourne Hall, Cokayne Ave
Ashbourne, Derbyshire DE6 1EJ England
Tel: (01335) 347349 Fax: (01335) 347303
e-mail: landmark@clara.net
web site: www.landmarkpublishing.co.uk

1st edition

ISBN 1-84306-144-9

Printed by Bath Press Ltd, Bath

Design & reproduction by James Allsopp

Cover captions:

Front cover: Anglian helmet
Back cover: Ivory Seal matrix; Clay pipe; Gold brooch; Leather shoe
Page 3: Anglian helmet

Contents

Foreword by HRH The Prince of Wales   6

Acknowledgements   7

The Historical and Archaeological Context   8

Plan of York   10

1. HEARTH AND HOME   13
   Make and mend — wooden bowls   14
   Head pots   16
   Glass ware   18
   'Bacchic' cup   20
   Slick-stones   21
   Storage pitcher   22
   Quern stones   23
   Wooden box lid with bone mounts   24
   Sewing equipment   25
   Roman pottery   28
   Wicker box lid   30
   Bucket   31
   Pestles and mortars   32
   Plant-holders   34
   Padlocks and keys   36
   Human waste   38
   Lavatory seat   39
   Mosaics   40

2. DRESS, JEWELLERY AND PERSONAL
   POSSESSIONS   45
   Gold brooches   46
   Strap-ends   48
   Buckles   49
   Jet and bone hairpins   50
   Ringed pins   51
   Silk cap   52
   Sock   54
   Leather shoes   55
   Amber pendants   57
   Gold, pearl and garnet ring   58
   Arm-rings   60
   Jet bracelet   61
   Glass beads   62
   Chatelaine   63
   Prick spurs   64
   Inlaid knives   66
   Composite combs   68
   Toilet implements   70
   Medical plate   72

3. GAMES, RECREATION AND LITERACY   75
   Bone skates   76
   Bowling ball   78
   Gaming board   80
   Dice   82
   Writing and literacy   84
   Wax tablets   86

Clay pipes   88
Pan pipes   90
Jew's harp   92
Tuning pegs and tuning key   94
Buzz bone   96
Queen Victoria medallion   97

4. CRAFT, TRADE AND INDUSTRY   99
   Seal   100
   Motif pieces   102
   Textile work   104
   Coin die and trial piece   108
   Samarkand coin   111
   Sugar mould   112
   Bones from skinning   114
   Cowrie shell   116
   Tools   117
   Balances and weights   120
   Knife handle   123
   Hone stones   124
   Bow saw   126
   Beaver bones   128

5. WEAPONS AND WARFARE   131
   Anglian helmet   132
   Seax sheaths   136
   Sword pommels   138
   Enamelled belt fitting   140
   Cheek-piece from a Roman helmet   141
   Archer's bracer   142
   Bow fragment   144

6. DEATH AND RITUAL   147
   Unguent bottle   148
   Oil lamp   149
   Burial pot   150
   Grave cover   152
   Rosary beads   154
   Gold and sapphire finger-ring   156
   Papal bulla   158
   Ampulla   160
   Chalice and paten   162
   Neolithic axe   164
   Christ Child stained glass   165
   Unfinished sculpture   166

Further information about the objects   168

Location of Objects   170

CLARENCE HOUSE

For many years now, I have had a particular interest in archaeology because I believe archaeological finds have the ability to combine the intrinsic beauty of objects themselves with the appeal of what they tell us about the way people lived in the past. I have certainly been heartened in recent years that there has been an enormous growth in public interest in archaeology – perhaps because of a number of enlightening television programmes allowing us access to the tools, and discoveries, of archaeologists.

This book, which celebrates the many treasures uncovered over the last thirty years by the excavations undertaken by the York Archaeological Trust, draws us into the day-to-day lives of our ancestors, whether in the Roman, Viking or Mediaeval periods, and I think none can fail to be intrigued by what is illustrated in the following pages.

As a Patron of the Trust's world-famous Viking excavations at Coppergate, York, and now as Patron of the Council for British Archaeology, I am delighted that the Trust has put together this book. It presents a fascinating range of those objects unearthed from below the streets of York, and I am sure it will extend the understanding and appreciation of archaeological finds to an ever-widening audience – and, I hope, might just encourage a new generation of people to become involved in this fascinating discipline and discover for themselves what remains of our forebears are waiting for discovery and interpretation...

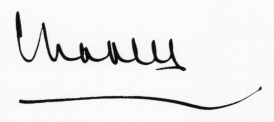

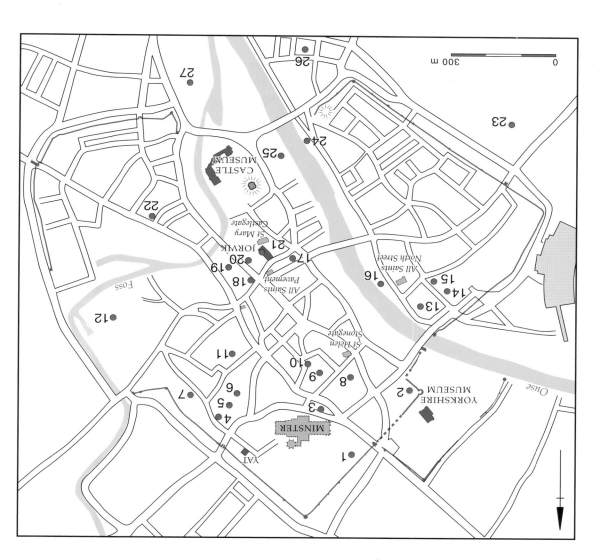

Plan of York showing the location of sites mentioned in the text

Plan of York

Excavation of the Victorian archaeological garden on the site of St Leonard's Hospital in the Museum Gardens, York.

Conqueror, the College of the Vicars Choral of York Minster at Bedern, the great Benedictine Abbey of St Mary and the city's finest guildhall, the Merchant Adventurers' Hall. We have relocated lost sites such as the medieval Jewish burial ground, the Gilbertine Priory of St Andrew, St Nicholas's leper hospital and several parish churches.

Post-Medieval York

In the 1530s, the Dissolution brought to ruins the mighty monastic houses which had dominated much of York, yet the city continued as an ecclesiastical, social and political centre. Faced by competition from Leeds and Hull, York lost its pre-eminent position as a trading centre by the 17th century but it remained a focus for commerce with busy river wharves and jetties. In the 19th century nonconformist religion flourished in York and a number of chapels were constructed, some of which survive today. The city remained a thriving social centre, and northern society flocked to the elegant 18th-century Assembly Rooms and other public buildings. Rowntree's chocolate factory opened in 1891 and by the late 19th century York was also a great railway centre. The Trust has excavated a number of post-medieval sites and buildings, including the Assembly Rooms. Amongst the evidence we have recovered for manufacturing in the city are late 17th-century pottery moulds for sugar refining and debris from 18th-century glass working.

The Historical and Archaeological Context

For most of the past 2,000 years York has been an important military, administrative, trad-ing, communication and religious centre. The citizens of York are rightly proud of their standing historic monuments — but still more of the city's heritage is waiting to be revealed beneath its narrow streets and ancient buildings. Buried remains are constantly coming to light as new buildings are erected, as streets, sewers and services are repaired, and as the city develops to meet modern needs.

Pre-Roman York

There are few traces of settlement in pre-Roman York, although artefacts such as flint axes dating to c.3000 BC have been found in the city. Aerial photography and excavation at Easingwold (north of York) and at Rawcliffe (just outside the city) suggests that the Vale of York was intensively occupied in late prehistoric times.

Roman York (*Eboracum*) c. AD 71–c.400

Founded as a fortress in AD 71, *Eboracum* became one of the most important cities of Roman Britain. Excavations by York Archaeological Trust have revealed the complex life of the fortress — with its barrack blocks, streets, bath houses and elaborate system of drains and sewers. In the civilian areas, public and private buildings have been discovered. These include town houses with mosaic floors, and possible bath houses and temples. We have also uncovered substantial river revetments (retaining structures) which were built to accommodate Roman ships bringing in goods from the rest of the empire.

Anglian York (*Eoforwic*) c.400–c.866

Little is known about York immediately after the withdrawal of the Roman garrisons from Britain in the early 5th century. There are very few traces of the Anglians who we know settled in the area during the 5th and 6th centuries. Our work has led, however, to a greater understanding of the later Anglian period. The world-famous 8th-century 'Coppergate helmet' was excavated in 1982, and the Trust discovered 7th- to 9th-century buildings near the River Foss in Fishergate in the mid 1980s.

Viking York (*Jorvik*) c.866–c.1067

The Vikings captured the city in 866 and there soon followed a tremendous boom in urban development. Excavations in Pavement and Coppergate uncovered material which attracted international interest and the so-called 'Viking Dig' brought thousands of visitors to York to see the excavations taking place. Part of Viking-Age Coppergate was revealed in all its detail — timber houses, workshops, fences, animal pens, privies, pits and wells. Objects indicated extensive international trade and highly skilled crafts and technologies. Wood, leather, textiles, and plant and animal remains, which do not normally survive, were recovered in great quantities, along with pottery, metalwork, bone, antler and all the debris of everyday life.

Medieval York c.1067–c.1550

After the Norman Conquest the city's appearance was changed dramatically, with castles, city walls, religious buildings, hospitals and town houses amongst the buildings erected. The Trust has excavated many of these, including the two castles established by William the

Acknowledgements

This book has been written and compiled by Christine Kyriacou, Frances Mee and Nicola Rogers. The text draws heavily on the work of many members of staff of York Archaeological Trust. It is based in great measure on fascicules on sites, artefacts and ecofacts published in *The Archaeology of York* series. The professional expertise of the authors of those fascicules used in the preparation of this book is gratefully acknowledged: Peter Addyman, David Brinklow, Esther Cameron, Ian Carlisle, Hilary Cool, Sara Donaghey, Rhona Finlayson, Pamela Graves, J.R.A. Greig, Allan Hall, Richard Hall, Dave Hooley, Harry Kenward, G. Lloyd-Morgan, Elizabeth Logan, Arthur MacGregor, John Magilton, Ailsa Mainman, Jason Monaghan, Carole Morris, Quita Mould, Joan Moulden, Terry O'Connor, Patrick Ottaway, Elizabeth Pirie, Julian D. Richards, Nicola Rogers, David Stocker, Dominic Tweddle, Penelope Walton Rogers and Dorian Williams.

No publication on artefacts would be possible without the skill and dedication of the conservators and curators who look after the objects once they have been recovered from the ground and ensure that they survive for future generations to research and enjoy. Thanks go to conservators Margaret Brooks, Kate Buckingham, Julie Jones, Sonia O'Connor, Ian Panter, Erica Paterson, Martin Read, Sue Rees and Jim Spriggs, and to finds assistants/curators Karen Adams, Susan Duffy, Renée Gajowskyj, Annie Jowett, Christine McDonnell, Bev Shaw and Gill Woolrich. Particular thanks are due to Christine McDonnell and Bev Shaw for making artefacts available for photography.

Elizabeth Hartley, Keeper of Archaeology at the Yorkshire Museum, provided access to artefacts in the museum's collection. Photographs of complete head pots and the Roman hairpiece with jet pins are reproduced by kind permission of York Museums Trust (Yorkshire Museum). Photographs of stained glass from York Minster are reproduced by kind permission of the Dean and Chapter of York: © Dean and Chapter of York. The photograph of the red squirrel is reproduced by kind permission of Allan Potts FRPS: © Allan Potts. The photograph of the beaver is reproduced by kind permission of Sharon T. Brown: www.BeaversWW.org.

All other photographs are by Mike Andrews and Simon I. Hill. The plan of York, the drawings and reconstruction diagrams are by Lesley Collett, some based on the work of former YAT illustrators.

Key to the Plan of York

1. Purey Cust Hospital
2. St Leonard's Hospital, Museum Gardens
3. 12 Minster Yard
4. 2 Aldwark
5. Bedern, College of Vicars Choral
6. Bedern Foundry
7. 21–33 Aldwark
8. 9 Blake Street
9. Coffee Yard
10. 12–18 Swinegate
11. St Andrewgate
12. Dundas Street, Hungate
13. Wellington Row
14. 5 Rougier Street
15. 24–30 Tanner Row
16. North Street
17. 28–9 High Ousegate
18. 6–8 Pavement
19. Merchant Adventurers' Hall
20. 22 Piccadilly
21. 16–22 Coppergate (and Coppergate watching brief)
22. 41–49 Walmgate
23. 35–41 Blossom Street
24. Pawson's Warehouse, Skeldergate
25. 1–2 Tower Street
26. Clementhorpe Nunnery
27. 46–54 Fishergate

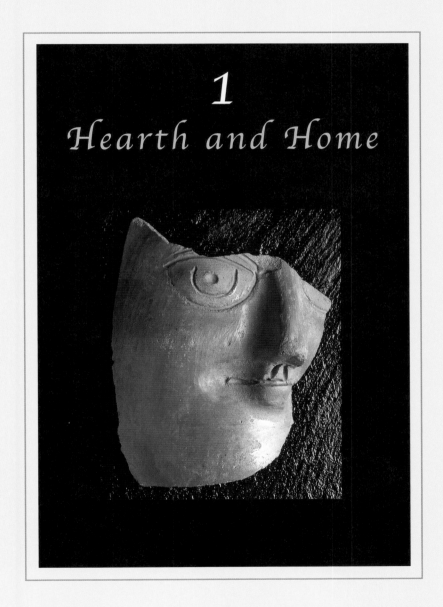

1
Hearth and Home

Make and mend — wooden bowls

Amongst the wonderful 10th-century oak buildings preserved in Coppergate and now recreated at the Jorvik Viking Centre was one in which unfinished bowls, lathe parts and masses of woodturning waste were all found. Fortunately many objects which don't normally survive, including those made of wood, have been protected by the special waterlogged soil conditions in some parts of York. The York Archaeological Wood Centre, which forms part of York Archaeological Trust, has gained an international reputation for the conservation and recording of wood and other materials from such anaerobic (lacking oxygen) land and marine environments.

The two bowls featured here are interesting as they were both made and subsequently mended in Viking times. The first, made of maple wood, has had a small split in the rim. A rectangular rim clip made of tin has been bent over the crack and held by an iron rivet on either side of the crack. Such clips were made to fit the bowl before they were fixed, and would never have been hammered into shape on the bowl. Internal grease and residue is clearly visible on this bowl, so we know it has been used to hold food. Rim clips found in early Anglo-Saxon graves often retain only a fragment of the wooden bowl but amazingly the outline and rim shape of the bowl are sometimes preserved in the cross-section of the clips.

The second bowl has been repaired with metal staples, an effective method of repairing wooden bowls since at least the early Anglo-Saxon period. Bowls repaired with metal staples were pierced by small holes on either side of the crack before the staple was put in, drawn tight and clenched to close the crack. This large birch bowl, 256mm in diameter, has a dark stained interior. The internal and external surfaces are also very worn and gouged. The bowl split in half in antiquity and was repaired by four iron staples, three clenched on the inside and one on the outside. Unfortunately it subsequently split again!

Bowls could have been repaired for a variety of reasons — their sentimental value, attraction, intrinsic usefulness or cost. Wooden bowls seem to have been relatively cheap to produce in rural areas where raw material was plentiful, but were probably more expensive in towns since a turner would have had to travel to woodland or import the raw material needed. Carole Morris, an expert on wood and woodworking, suggests that some repaired bowls that split during seasoning may actually have been sold as 'seconds'. Since such bowls would have been so time-consuming to make, it is not surprising that they were often so beautifully repaired.

Woodland of the type which would have existed around York in Anglo-Scandinavian times

Above: Tenth-century bowl repaired with a metal rim clip (diameter 193mm)
Below: Tenth-century bowl repaired with metal staples (diameter 256mm)

A reminder of the international nature of the Roman Empire comes in the form of these wonderful head pots which were initially made in York by soldier-potters from North Africa. These potters had been brought to Britain by the Emperor Severus, and seem to have manufactured the pots around AD 211–12 when the Imperial family was in York.

Third-century head pot fragment from Wellington Row, probably female. The eyes and eyebrows have been incised, the nose, mouth and chin formed of added clay (maximum width 140mm)

Parts of some 50 head pots have been found in York. The whole vessel below the rim was fashioned in the form of a head and neck, with naturalistic facial features and hair. They were wheel-thrown and then sculpted into the shape of a human face. The finest vessels had their features formed by pressing or pinching the clay, but cruder examples were simply made by adding clay to the thrown pot. The pots were then incised to add detail and pick out features such as eyes and nostrils. The mouth is usually small and the cheeks full. Eyebrows are suggested by incised dots, and ears are concealed below the hair, which is denoted by incising or combing. The material is similar to oxidised Ebor ware, the local material used for cooking vessels, although the colour is often pinker, giving a flesh-tinted vessel in keeping with the form of the pot.

Who were the face pots intended to represent? They are normally female, and may have been idealised portraits of the owners of the pots or their spouses. However, the hair styles of many are reminiscent of those of Severus' Syrian wife, Julia Domna, who may have acted as inspiration. Julia Domna stayed in York with Severus, and her hair creations would also have been familiar to York's inhabitants through the coinage and effigies of the time. Hairstyle apart, facial details of several vessels — aquiline nose, prominent eyes and wide-arched brow — are thought to be compatible with her Syrian origin.

What was the function of the head pots? Although some have been found with burials, they are distributed widely both inside and outside the Roman fortress, suggesting that their function was not solely funerary. They may have had a ritual rather than funerary function, perhaps placed in household shrines, or to hold libations (drink offerings to the gods). Their presence in a small number of graves may merely indicate that they were treasured possessions rather than part of the funerary rite. Who, after all, would not wish to be accompanied to the grave by such handsome images!

Right: Third-century female head pot fragment from 24–30 Tanner Row, with incised features and aquiline nose (maximum height 114mm)

Bottom left: Complete female head pot found in York cemetery in 1888 (height 300mm). Reproduced by courtesy of York Museums Trust (Yorkshire Museum)

Bottom right: Male head pot found in Priory Street in the 19th century (height 250mm). Reproduced by courtesy of York Museums Trust (Yorkshire Museum)

Roman glass was widely used all over the Roman Empire, in York as elsewhere. Little is known about the glass industry between the decline of the Roman Empire and the 1200s, and it was not until the 1500s that glassmaking became important in England. Medieval glass vessels seem to have been imported into York from Germany, France, Italy, Spain and the eastern Mediterranean.

Glass is found in relatively small quantities during excavations. In Roman times this was because of the equivalent of bottle banks! Broken glass was deliberately collected for recycling as the Romans found out that, when making glass from the raw ingredients of sand and an alkali, the addition of broken glass lowered the temperature at which melting took place and thus saved fuel.

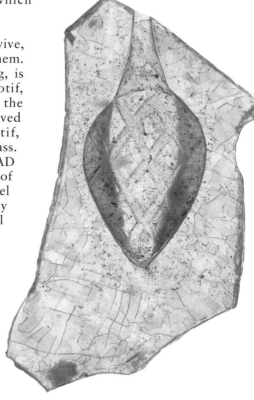

As a result, only fragments of glass tend to survive, but a surprising amount can be learnt from them. This piece from Blake Street, just 36mm long, is extraordinarily rare as the pointed oval motif, possibly of an acorn, has been raised above the surface by a narrow spine of glass. This was achieved by undercutting the glass around the motif, removing in places approximately 10mm of glass. What we have is a fragment of a 1st-century AD 'cage cup', one of the most luxurious products of the Roman glass industry, in which a glass vessel was covered with a lattice or cage which was only connected to the main body of the vessel by small bridges, the rest of the glass having been ground away. From where it was found, it seems that this vessel may have been in use for more than 100 years before it was broken.

Above: Rare 'cage cup' glass fragment, 1st century AD (length 36mm)

Left: Blue glass fragment, 13th–14th century (width 24mm)

The second fragment featured opposite, 24mm across, is from the flattened centre of a bowl or goblet from Bedern, 13th- or 14th-century in style. It is blue glass with black painted decoration. This decoration consists of a circular border with serrated outer edges and a six-pointed hexagram (or possibly a pentagram) star made up of two interlacing triangles within the border. There is a foliate decoration within and between the points of the star. The centre of the star has not survived. Hexagrams and pentagrams had a symbolic significance in the Near East where they represented the Seal of Solomon and were used as protective talismans, but the York example is thought to be simply decorative. Vessels made of blue glass are relatively rare in medieval Europe, and the York bowl would thus have been distinctive and valuable.

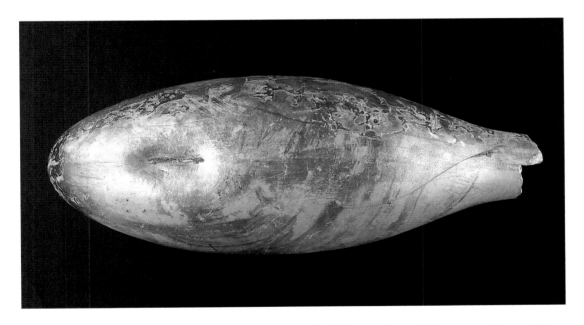

An interesting glass bottle (length 190mm) unearthed during the training excavation at the medieval St Leonard's Hospital. It was called a 'Thompson's bomb' after its inventor. The curved shape means that the bottle cannot stand upright, and this prevents the cork from drying off and popping out

'Bacchic' cup

This vessel is extraordinarily rare. Excavators at Wellington Row in 1987 unearthed a handful of grey-white pieces of pottery with a dark green glaze. After cleaning, the Conservation Department was able to join most of the fragments to produce one of the most complete examples of its type known from Britain. It was found in a ditch dated to c.AD 225, but similarity to a vessel in Cologne suggests that it may have been made in the previous century.

What we have is the upper part of a 'cantharus', a two-handled drinking cup modelled on metal prototypes that would have had a pedestal base, rather like a modern football trophy. The form is eastern in origin, and may have been imported from the Rhineland. Decoration was added to the vessel prior to glazing and consists of 'appliqué' figures, produced in moulds and then individually stuck onto the pot. Detail was added using liquid clay. This would have been very time-consuming and the pot would clearly have been expensive.

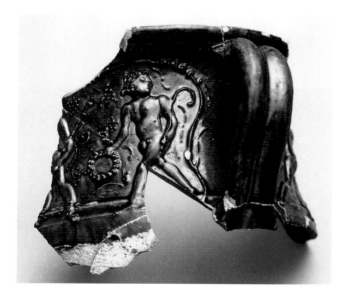

Several figures feature on the pot, two of whom survive in considerable detail. They are naked, curly-haired men, probably satyrs. One bears a bunch of grapes in his left hand and perhaps another implement in his right. The other carries a laurel wreath in his right hand and what may be a shepherd's crook in his left. The whole scene is set in a grove of vines. The design is clearly connected with the cult of the god Bacchus, the god of wine and the centre of certain fertility rites. Members of the Bacchic cult took part in notorious orgiastic revels, and the cult was suppressed in the 1st century BC because of the public disturbances it caused. It re-emerged in the 1st century AD as a respectable 'mystery' religion and persisted until the 4th century.

Roman pottery expert Jason Monaghan describes the scene on this vessel as 'restrained and tasteful' and 'lacking the touch of sinister lewdness evident in the harder core of Bacchic art'. Thus its presence does not necessarily point to a Bacchic cult in York. It was more likely to have been simply a drinking cup with particularly appropriate decoration.

Two views of a green-glazed 'Bacchic' cup from the late 2nd or 3rd century AD (maximum height 100mm)

Slick-stones

These objects are the Viking equivalent of today's hand irons! They are called slick-stones or linen-smoothers, and were used as far back as the Roman period in the manufacture and laundering of cloth. They disappeared when the Romans left northern Europe, and reappeared at the end of the 9th century. By the 10th century they were in common use throughout north-west Europe. They are made of glass or stone. They are generally thought to have been used with the whalebone boards carved with heads which are found in Viking graves (although only in Birka, Sweden, have both slick-stones and smoothing boards been found together).

Several stone slick-stones have been identified from the Coppergate site in York (the three on the right of the picture). Their fabric is similar to that of the glass slick-stones. When viewed under a microscope, one example was seen to have fine scratch marks on the surface. These radiated out from the centre as if the stone had been used in a back and forth action, rather than round and round. Only one stone example has so far been recorded from elsewhere in Anglo-Saxon England, although it is possible that stone slick-stones may have been overlooked on archaeological sites. The Coppergate evidence suggests that stone slick-stones were ousted by glass slick-stones in the 10th century.

Several dozen fragments of glass slick-stones, ranging in date from the 10th to the 13th century, have been found in York. They seem to have been circular and relatively flat or slightly domed, with a depression on the back formed during the manufacturing process. Again, when viewed under a microscope, the scratches suggest a back and forth motion. X-ray surface analysis has shown that several of the well-preserved examples have a high lead content. The relatively common black or dark green colour is due to high levels of iron.

Above: Viking-Age slick-stones of glass and stone (diameter of example on the far right 73mm)

Below: Photomicrograph of fine scratches on a slick-stone

Slick-stones were a simple product for the glass-worker to make, as they merely required molten glass to be rotated on a rod. A 10th-century workshop using high-lead glass has been identified in Coppergate, and by the 12th century there was another in the Shambles. Thus any laundress or needlewoman needing a smoother would probably not have had far to go. One can only wonder how effective they were!

Storage pitcher

Rough calculations of the total amount of pottery from the excavations at Coppergate between 1976 and 1981 indicate that some 230,000 vessel fragments were unearthed, weighing some 4.6 tons! Probably about two-thirds date from the Viking period, and all demanded attention. A mammoth task!

Imagine the satisfaction, though, of piecing together a large spouted Viking-Age pitcher such as this one. In all, 170 pieces of it were found. The pitcher is almost half a metre high, and has three plain strap handles round the rim and four subsidiary handles set on the shoulder which have been decorated with thumb marks. Applied clay stripes, also carefully decorated with thumb marks, run vertically. There is a further thumbed strip set on the rim, probably to thicken and strengthen it. The vessel must have been extraordinarily heavy to move or pour from when full of liquid. What liquid it used to hold is unknown, though it may have been used in brewing.

The pitcher is Torksey-type ware, named after the site of a small Anglo-Scandinavian borough close to the River Trent just north of Lincoln. Products of the Torksey kilns included pots, bowls, lamps, storage jars and pitchers. Decoration was fairly limited — often a thumbed, piecrust-effect rim on cooking pots, or applied thumbed-strip decoration as on the Coppergate pitcher. The trade from Torksey would have come by river, down the Trent to the Humber and then up the Ouse to York. It must have been encouraged by the development of markets in York, and probably lasted from the early 10th to the early 12th century. Previously, York's pottery would have been produced locally, in standard forms and sizes. Perhaps it was the handsome thumbed adornment or multiple handles that caught the eye of the purchaser of this fine vessel!

Tenth- or eleventh-century pitcher of Torksey-type ware (height 440mm)

Quern stones

Among the most intriguing finds from excavations on the site of an old glass factory in Fishergate were the rotary querns or millstones — 123 quern fragments and, best of all, a complete 11th- or 12th-century rotary quern, comprising both upper and lower stones, found in a pit and looking much as it would have done on the day it was discarded. Such hand querns were domestic utensils which were important in food preparation, and were originally used to grind grain to make flour.

The stones needed no special conservation treatment, just a wash and brush to clean them up. A geologist identified the stone as a coarse-grained sandstone, typically found in Millstone Grit which occurs in the Pennines. The nearest outcrops to York are in the Harrogate region. Both stones had smooth areas on the surfaces which ground against each other. Both had a large central perforation for a spindle around which the upper stone was turned. The upper stone also had a flange around the perforation on its upper face which acted as a funnel for the grain, and grooves each side on the lower surface which may have originally held a 'rynd', now lost. The rynd would have been a strip, perhaps of wood, with a central hole which fitted over the spindle.

Most of the other quern fragments excavated on the site were made of lava, found especially in the Mayen area of Germany, and imported for making querns. This particular type of stone maintained its roughness despite constant use, making it an ideal surface on which to grind grain.

Why were these serviceable, vital utensils, made from materials quarried 30 or more miles away and then specially fashioned for their purpose, simply abandoned? We know that this type of grinding stone went out of use early in the medieval period, because during the 12th century their use was prohibited, following the introduction of watermills. Grain had to be ground at the lord of the manor's mills where dues had to be paid, so perhaps the explanation lies here.

Above: Pair of rotary quern stones as found by archaeologists (scale unit 100mm). Both stones were approximately 400mm in diameter

Left: Reconstruction drawing showing how querns were used

A remarkable 11th-century wooden box lid was found in the wet soils of Coppergate, associated with a wooden building which stood on the site just before the Norman Conquest. It is about 340mm long and 140mm wide, and the entire top surface is covered with strips of decorated bone.

The wood was very degraded, so the object had to be immersed in a solution of polyethylene glycol, a water-soluble polymer that gradually displaced the ground water holding it together. Once dry, the polymer hardened, strengthening the fragile cell structure of the wood. The bone mounts needed little treatment other than cleaning.

The wood was found to be a single piece of oak about 6mm thick. Nineteen bone mounts had been attached to the top using iron rivets. The mounts were made from split cattle rib bones and a shoulder-blade, cut to size and shape. Many of the mounts were decorated with a zigzag pattern of double lines composed of repeated dots, made using a double-pointed punch. Other strips were decorated with parallel lines and ring-and-dot motifs in different combinations.

Fragments from 11th- and 12th-century contexts in York, Dublin and elsewhere suggest that this type of decoration was popular at this time. On the Continent, cathedral treasuries house complete caskets mounted with bone or ivory strips which might have held relics and other valuables. The examples from York would have been used for small precious belongings such as coins, jewellery or other personal items. The box lid from Coppergate is now on display in the Jorvik Viking Centre, where visitors can admire the handiwork of the original craftsman thanks to the painstaking and careful work of the archaeological conservators.

Above: Box lid in the ground before it was lifted by archaeologists
Below: Eleventh-century wooden box lid covered with strips of decorated bone (length 336mm)

Sewing equipment

In medieval York, as elsewhere in England, needlework was a common domestic activity, undertaken by the women, or female servants, of the house. As the objects here show, most of the tools involved in cutting and stitching are almost exactly the same as those in use today. There are one or two exceptions, however, and some perhaps surprising variations on modern equipment.

Needles were made of either iron or copper alloy, but the choice of metal used does not seem to have been of any particular significance. Needles of both metals ranged in length and thickness — most would have been used in ordinary needlework, such as the needles shown here, but finer needles might have been used perhaps for sewing silk, while coarser needles may have been used to stitch sacking. Needles are occasionally found which have a triangular cross-section. These would have been used to make repairs to leather garments.

Continued overleaf

A group of needles, all made of copper alloy with the exception of the one on the far right which is of iron (length of centre needle 109mm)

The needles with open-ended eyes at each end are netting needles. These would have been used to make hairnets of knotted silk mesh, which were particularly popular amongst women in the 13th and 14th centuries, and were worn at the back of the head. The diagram shows how the mesh was made using a netting needle. The silk yarn was wound lengthways between the forked ends of the needle which was used to produce a series of loops.

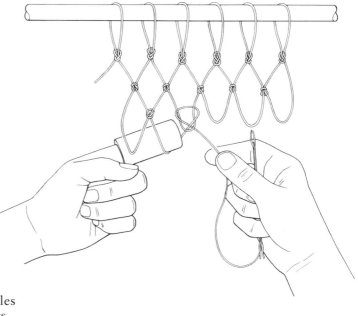

Knotted mesh being made with a netting needle. The mesh has been drawn larger than life, to show the technique

The medieval iron scissors are a rare archaeological find, recovered from a 14th-century deposit at Bedern. Shears of a similar form to those used in sheep shearing are found more frequently, and some of the smaller examples may have been used like scissors.

As with the needles, the form of medieval thimbles is exactly like those of today, although they were mostly handmade, rather than machine-made. Unusually, this thimble was found to have a separate inner lining made from a strip of leather which had been sewn into a dome shape. This is one of only two known from the whole of medieval England, the other having been found in south Yorkshire. The lack of other such linings may be the result of their being made of organic materials, which generally disintegrate in the soil. Many seamstresses and tailors may have used linings to provide padding on painful nails or joints, or to make a better fit for their fingers.

Medieval iron scissors from Bedern (length 125mm)

Two views of the thimble with a leather lining (diameter 22mm)

Vast quantities of Roman and later pottery are found every time excavations take place in York. Roman pottery found includes the ubiquitous red samian pottery, imported from northern and later from central France, which was standard tableware in the 1st and 2nd century AD. Ebor ware, actually made in York as its name signifies (*Eboracum* is the Roman name for York), is also commonly found in the city.

Another type, which provides a good example of regional trade, is Crambeck pottery which was produced near Crambeck in North Yorkshire. It was distributed all across northern Britain during the 4th century AD, and comes in grey, red and white colours. The examples of Crambeck ware illustrated here are known as 'parchment ware', which is a hard and brittle fabric, either white or buff-coloured. The basic white Crambeck fabric was given an off-white 'parchment' wash which could then be over-painted with red designs, normally in bands around the vessel consisting of plain stripes or repeating geometric forms.

Above: Samian cups found at Blake Street, late 1st century AD (cup diameter 85mm)

Below: Ebor ware flagon from Blake Street, late 1st century AD (height 265mm)

The Crambeck fragment with the painted figure featured here was found in Coppergate. The figure may be a warrior wearing a tunic and belt, brandishing a sword in his right hand, with a burning brand or club in his left. Alternatively, he may be a smith-god, wearing an apron, with his right hand raising a hammer and his left holding tongs. The fragment is part of a plate.

The other piece with concentric circles was originally from a plate or bowl, but had been trimmed to create a playing counter. Someone obviously had an eye for a pleasing design!

Crambeck
'parchment'
ware from the
4th century AD,
trimmed as a
counter (width
48mm)

Crambeck
'parchment'
ware with
painted warrior
or smith-god
(maximum
height 83mm)

Wicker box lid

The wet soils of Coppergate preserved many organic items including a box lid woven from willow. It looks just like part of a modern laundry basket but it is 700 years old and the product of a skilled medieval craftsman. It was recovered, together with some old shoes, from an excavated cellar within the remains a timber-framed building. The building seems to have been an ordinary residence rather than a workshop.

Medieval wicker box lid as it was found in the ground (maximum length 330mm)

This is a rare and interesting object. When discovered the lid had been squashed out of shape by the soil around it and was very soft and fragile. The challenge was to lift the lid without further damage so that it could be conserved and studied. The on-site conservation team carefully removed most of the dirt from its upper surface. The lid was then undercut and successfully block-lifted from the ground (that is, lifted along with rigid foam or supporting material to give added support) and taken to the laboratory.

What was discovered was a unique example of skilled woodworking and basketry techniques of the 13th or 14th century. A willow frame with jointed corners contained thin wooden slats retained in slots cut into the sides of the frame. Spaces between the slats were then filled with tightly packed woven willow rods. In the middle were the remains of a plaited willow handle. There was no metal at all in the lid: even the hinges were probably willow rods or another organic material which threaded through a hole in the side of the wooden frame.

The lid would originally have been about 55–60cm long and just over 27cm wide, but the depth of the box it covered cannot be estimated. The walls of the box might have been of the same construction as the lid or possibly of solid wood planks.

No other lid of this type is known in England or Europe but the technique of mortice and tenon construction (where two pieces of wood are joined at right angles with a hole or slot in one piece, into which the other piece is inserted) goes back many centuries. We can only guess at the use of the box. Willow is still popular for storing household linen so perhaps we should imagine it in the corner of a room, away from the damp, full of fine linen interleaved with lavender and other sweet-smelling herbs.

Bucket

Probably the most perfectly preserved medieval bucket in Britain was found at the bottom of a medieval well at Coppergate in York. The well itself was lined with a barrel (or cask) and the waterlogged conditions inside the well were ideal for the preservation of both the wooden bucket and its iron chain and fittings.

Conservators found that the bucket was made of nine oak uprights, called staves, which were bound together by three iron bands. A handle was fixed through holes pierced in two longer staves whose rounded ends extended beyond the rim. These holes had been reinforced with iron plates to take the weight from a chain which was attached to the handle using a swivelling mechanism.

The well and the bucket are both of early 15th-century date. This date is based on the pottery which was found with the bucket and on the position of the well in relation to the other layers on site. The bucket would have been made by a specialist cooper. Coopers probably worked outside the city in woodland areas, close to their raw materials, and would have brought their products to sell in town markets.

Buckets of this type were made in a range of sizes and had many uses. This one had clearly been used to raise water from the well. Perhaps the last time it was used the chain broke or the water-hauler let the bucket fall by accident. Whatever the circumstances, it lay there buried over three metres deep and perfectly preserved for 600 years until archaeologists uncovered it.

Above: Bucket at the bottom of a medieval well (scale unit 10cm)

Left: Wooden bucket with iron fittings after conservation (height 424mm)

Pestles and mortars

It may be surprising to learn that one of the most commonly recovered items of medieval kitchen equipment on excavations is the mortar. Just as today, these tough stone vessels were used with pestles to grind various foodstuffs, although judging by recipes which survive from the period, grinding of a much greater variety of ingredients was required than we would expect in our own kitchens.

Of course, one reason why mortars survive for hundreds of years under the ground is because they were made of a very durable material. When no longer required for food preparation — perhaps because they had finally broken — fragments of mortars did not go to waste, but were re-used as rubble in walls or hearths. A study of more than twenty mortar fragments found in York noted that the stone type most commonly used was Magnesian Limestone which is found along the western edge of the Vale of York, the nearest source to the city itself being some ten miles away in the Tadcaster-Wetherby area. The mortar base illustrated on page 33 is of this stone type. Locally sourced sandstone was also favoured, but other more distant

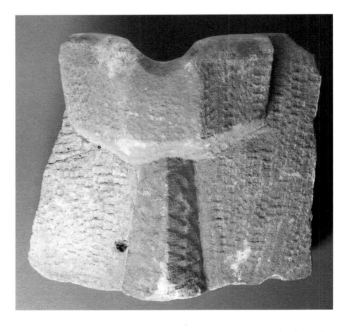

sources of stone were sometimes employed. The second mortar featured here, and also the pestle fragment, are of limestone that probably came from Dorset; perhaps this stone was thought to be superior to the local limestone, and worth transporting over quite a distance.

Most of the mortar fragments recovered share certain features such as lugs or lips with runnels, moulded projections, and ribs on the wall exteriors. As well as providing strength to the body of the mortar, the ribs and lips may have enabled the mortar to be set into a table top, and kept in a firm position, allowing both hands to be used for grinding. Unlike mortars, stone pestles are rarely recovered, but medieval illustrations of mortars in use sometimes show long, possibly wooden, pestles. Such wooden pestles would be far less likely to survive burial for hundreds of years than stone objects.

So, what sort of foodstuffs might have been ground in these mortars? Well, surviving recipes suggest ingredients of all sorts could be prepared in such vessels. Meat such as pork was often ground up to make meatballs, as in a 13th-century recipe which suggests making pork meatballs to resemble oranges, and sprinkling them with sugar when cooked! Nuts were also ground up. Almond milk, made with ground almonds and sugar or honey, for example, was popular in the 15th century, and was used with finely ground fish such as haddock — also ground in the mortar — to make *Mortrose of Fyshe*, the word *mortrose* meaning mortar, from the vessel in which it was prepared.

Above: Mortar fragment with external rib from Bedern (height 25mm)

Incomplete stone mortar from Coppergate and stone pestle from Bedern (length of pestle 56mm)

Plant-holders

Gardening is a popular activity in York today, and the discovery of pieces of medieval flowerpots or plant-holders has provided clear evidence of similar activity in the medieval city. Gardening then, as now, would have been for culinary use and for pleasure, although growing flowers could also have been for profit — a flower market in Norwich is recorded as early as the 14th century. In medieval times gardening for medicinal purposes was also important.

Part of a medieval ceramic plant-holder from Coppergate with a human face between two handles

The Coppergate fragment featured here is about 100mm wide. It has part of a human face between two of the handles, surrounded by incised combed wavy lines and set within an inverted horseshoe-shaped applied thumbed strip. Internal as well as external surfaces of such pots were glazed. All the medieval plant-holders found in York seem to have had three handles and were so heavy that they must have been made in several pieces. The surviving pieces of one example weigh over 2.5kg — and this represents less than two-thirds of the top of the vessel and only a small part of one of the three handles! In all the York examples, the join between the top and bottom halves is evident, albeit masked by an applied thumbed strip. One side of such planters may have been designed to be placed against a wall.

Although there are medieval illustrations showing flowers, particularly lilies, growing in ceramic garden pots very similar to those sold in garden centres today, surviving ceramic garden furniture is rare before the 18th century. Most such vessels have been identified largely from rims and handles; surprisingly, the shape of the bottom of many such pots is still somewhat speculative. It is similarity to post-medieval forms that suggests that these early examples were ornamental plant-holders. Nowadays much more attention is being paid to gardens than in the past, and the discovery and proper identification of such vessels is sure to enhance our understanding of gardening in medieval times.

Top of a medieval ceramic plant-holder from the site of the College of Vicars Choral, Bedern

Judging by the numbers of keys and locks recovered from Coppergate, security of property and possessions was as high a priority for the Viking-Age inhabitants of York as it is for us today. Parts of locks that would have been fixed to doors or chests, padlocks of two different forms and the keys that went with them have all been recovered. All were made of iron. Here is a selection of keys that would have opened padlocks and the remains of a padlock itself.

Two forms of padlock are known from this period — the box padlock and the barrel padlock. As their names suggest, the box padlock had a cube-shaped body, while the barrel padlock was tubular. Box padlocks themselves are rarely recovered, but an almost complete box padlock key (below at left) with a decoratively made stem and a rectangular bit was recovered from Viking-Age levels at Coppergate.

Barrel padlocks came in two forms, the main difference being the point at which the key entered the lock. Unlike modern padlocks which usually have the key hole on the front, on these the key entered through a hole either in one end or in the side. The barrel padlock in the photograph has the key hole in one end. It has been decorated with applied metal strips, some of which have been twisted in a wave pattern. The key with the angled up bit (below, centre) would have opened a padlock similar to this.

The other key (below at right) would have operated a barrel padlock with a key hole in the side, as shown in the reconstruction drawing.

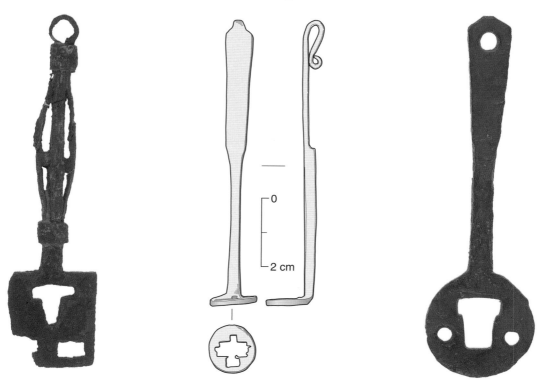

Left, key for a box padlock (length 79mm); centre, key with an angled up bit for a barrel padlock; right, key for a barrel padlock (length 55mm)

Above: Barrel padlock from Coppergate (length 86mm)

Below: Reconstruction drawing showing how a barrel padlock with the key entering from the side would be opened

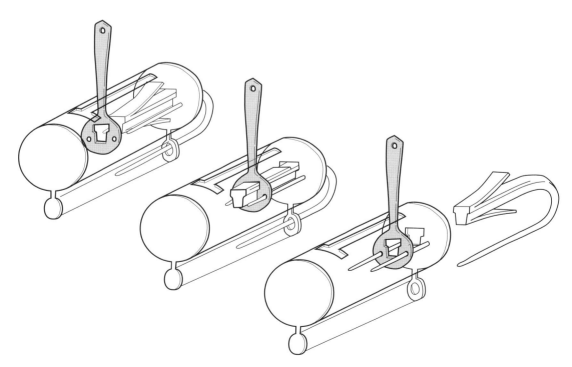

Sometimes a find turns out to be something quite different from what was first thought. Excavation of Viking-Age levels during construction of bank vaults at Lloyds Bank, Pavement, in 1972 produced what was thought to be a piece of metalworking slag. Closer examination told us otherwise — and gave a whole new meaning to the term 'making a deposit'!

The hard brittle object almost 20cm long and 5cm wide turned out to be mineralised Viking-Age human faeces, a stool or coprolite. A team of scientists rolled up their sleeves and prepared to see what this most direct human by-product had to tell us. After all, 'we are what we eat', and there was a lot we could learn.

A sample of the hard object had first to be softened and pulled apart, by being soaked in dilute hydrochloric acid. This produced a brown liquid containing particles of different sizes which were separated using sieves. The different parts were then studied under a microscope. These studies revealed that the meal eaten by the producer of the stool had included cereal bran and other unidentified organic matter. This confirms other forms of evidence which suggest that diet at this time included cereals as well as meat, fish, shellfish, fruit and nuts. In addition, however, there were many eggs of intestinal parasites — gut worms of the types known as whipworm and maw-worm. These are only regularly found together in pig or man, and the form of this stool suggests that it was human.

Calculations, based on the number of eggs recovered, showed that the individual was infested with a small number of maw-worms and several hundred whipworms. By today's standards this would be a heavy infection. Although well within the limits of human tolerance, the individual almost certainly had stomach ache at times!

Above: Viking-Age human excrement from 6–8 Pavement, rich in bran and parasite eggs

Right: Egg from the parasite whipworm from the Pavement stool

Lavatory seat

Some objects found by archaeologists are instantly recognisable; their shape and function have not changed for thousands of years. The wet soils of Coppergate in York perfectly preserved two such objects, which are unmistakably toilet seats, from levels which date them to the 12th century.

These 900-year-old seats are both made of thick oak planks about one metre in length. They are the seats from medieval garderobes which were made of a box or panel construction. One was found in a pit which might have been the cesspit over which it was originally used.

The toilet seats were conserved after being lifted from the soil by being immersed in polyethylene glycol, a water-soluble polymer commonly used in the cosmetics and pharmaceutical industries today. The conservation process for these fragile wooden seats took approximately three years to complete.

One side of the seat was shaped (chamfered). Often such chamfering allowed a circular lid to be fitted snugly over the hole. The hole itself would have been made by incising a circle of the required size on the surface of the plank and then boring small holes through the plank very close together. When the last hole was made the centre could then easily be cut through with a chisel. It could then be smoothed down to minimise the risk of splinters!

Both the York examples are 'single holers' but there are medieval examples, including one of slightly earlier date from London, with three holes side by side in a single plank. Such friendly arrangements continued in rural areas of England until quite recent times.

Above: Drawing of a 'triple holer'

Right:
Twelfth-century wooden toilet seat that had fallen into a cesspit (scale unit 10cm)

York was part of the Roman Empire for over 300 years after the 9th Legion first set foot in the city in AD 71. In both buildings and artefacts we often find traces of ancient Roman life, none more typically Roman, perhaps, than the mosaic floors.

Mosaics came into common use from the 2nd century AD, and would decorate the dining room and other principal rooms of the homes of wealthy people. Designs were probably taken from pattern books and included geometric patterns, fish, animals and mythological subjects. It seems that there was a firm of mosaicists working in York or Aldborough in the late 3rd century AD.

The first Roman mosaic pictured here, originally located by the Victorians in 1851, was excavated on the site of the Benedictine nunnery in Clementhorpe. It dates from the 4th century AD and has a design of geometric patterns, incorporating crescent shapes, knots and an intricate interlaced border of six-stranded guilloche (an ornament which imitates braided ribbons). Nothing remains of the central square that this border would have surrounded. The mosaic was made up of different types of material in red (tile), beige (limestone), pink (baked limestone), light brown (sandstone), dark grey (slate), black (jet or shale) and white (the background chalk).

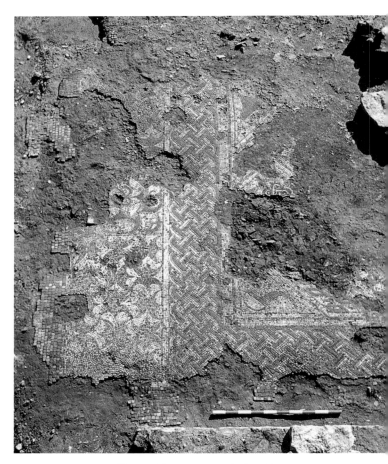

Clementhorpe mosaic in situ

After excavation, the Clementhorpe mosaic was lifted for transportation to the Yorkshire Museum. A facing fabric of gauze was stuck to the surface with adhesive, and it was undercut with long slaters' knives to remove all the now-soft Roman mortar. It was divided into convenient sections and slid onto boards for removal. At the conservation laboratory the sections were turned over and any remaining mortar was removed. The sections were then backed with modern support materials. Turned the right way over again, the adhesive was dissolved so the facing gauze could be removed. The surface of the mosaic was then thoroughly cleaned, ready for display.

Right: Preparing the Clementhorpe mosaic for removal

Below: Lifting the Clementhorpe mosaic

Mosaic pavement in situ at Aldwark (scale unit 0.1m)

The second Roman mosaic, also 4th-century in date, survived as it had been sealed under the floors of the medieval church of St Helen-on-the-Walls in Aldwark. It seems to have been the pavement of a corridor. It comprises a 2.2m by 2m rectangular panel with a head at the centre encircled originally by four strips of guilloche, then dark grey lozenges with light grey centres with small chessboard patterns in the corners, followed by a band of triangles of red and beige, surrounded by a broad band of red. On the right side a large chessboard pattern in red and beige extends for at least 2.8m.

The head, which is thought to be of a female, has been executed in pink tesserae (see p.43). The greater part of the face and hair, as well as part of the neck and right shoulder, survive. There are white highlights on the left cheekbone, down the right side of the nose and elsewhere, whilst shadows down the left side of the face and neck and under the chin are in brown. The eyes are each depicted by a single rounded black tessera. The hair is of grey and purple stripes with curls about both ears. The mosaic had been patched in antiquity.

The rather more modern mosaic featured here is that of the attractive 19th-century threshold of the Old Malt Shovel Inn, which used to be opposite the junction of Walmgate and Merchantgate until its demolition in the 1960s. To lift this, the surface was first thoroughly washed with water and detergent, and left to dry in the sun. It was then painted with thick layers of a reversible adhesive, and overlaid with several layers of nylon gauze applied in broad strips at right angles to each other and overlapping the edges of the mosaic. The threshold was then undermined and long stout timbers were inserted beneath the cement and rubble so that the entire panel could be lifted onto a pallet to be transported to the Castle Museum.

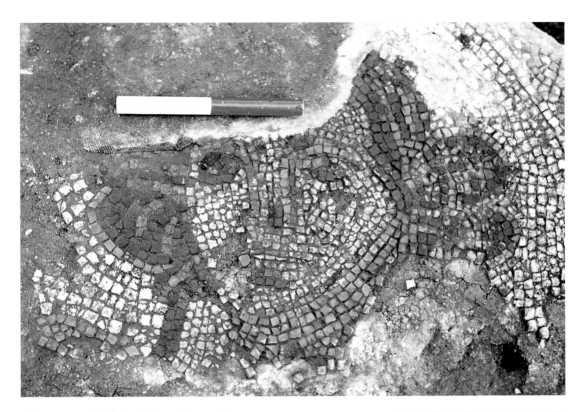

Above: Detail of the Aldwark mosaic showing the female face

Right: Old Malt Shovel Inn mosaic threshold

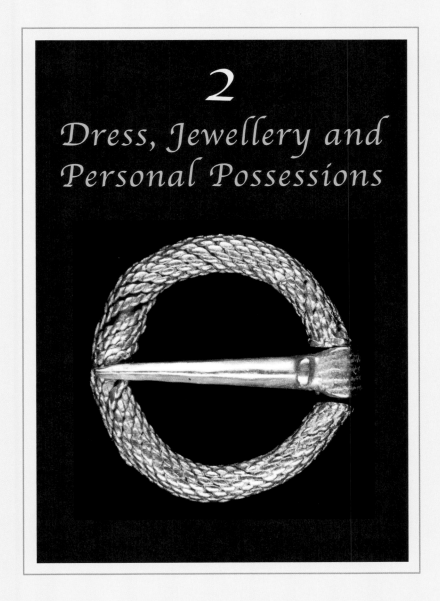

2
Dress, Jewellery and Personal Possessions

Gold objects are very rare archaeological recoveries — gold has always been a very valuable metal and not one to be discarded lightly. Occasionally, however, gold items are found, mostly small personal possessions which were presumably accidentally lost. The gold objects seen here are medieval annular (ring-like) brooches. Such brooches were used as fasteners for clothing and as decorative ornaments, and contemporary illustrations show that they were worn mainly at the neck and by both men and women. Most were made of base metals, such as copper and lead alloys, making them affordable for many, but only people of considerable wealth could have bought gold brooches such as those illustrated here.

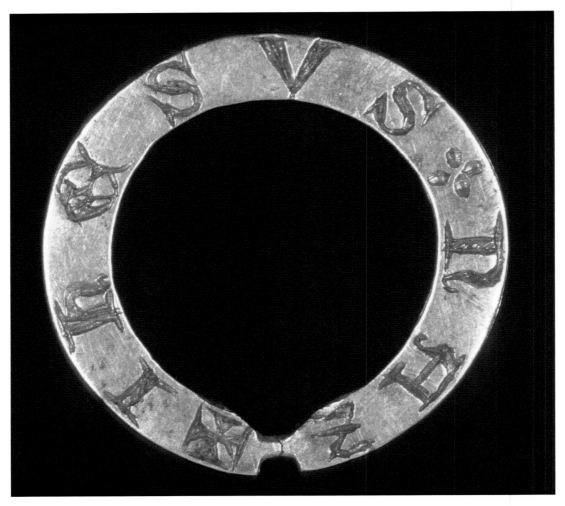

Inscribed gold brooch from the Merchant Adventurers' Hall (diameter 21mm)

One brooch has lost its pin, but it can be identified as an annular brooch by the constriction on the frame, around which the pin would have been looped. It is inscribed *IHESUS NAZ* in Lombardic lettering on one face, representing the name Jesus of Nazareth. This inscription, commonly used on medieval jewellery, was thought to be a protection against sudden death. In fact, the brooches themselves were often believed to have special powers. A 13th-century gold brooch found at Writtle in Essex was inscribed 'I am a brooch to guard the breast, so that no ruffian may put his hand there'! The York brooch was recovered during excavations at the Merchant Adventurers' Hall, and probably dates to the 14th century. A group of merchants bought a block of land on Fossgate in 1356, and tree-ring dating of timbers suggests that the first hall was probably erected by 1361, so perhaps this brooch belonged to one of these first merchant adventurers.

The other brooch is made of decoratively twisted multi-strand gold wire and retains its pin, which appears to have a gripping or clasped hand design at the point where it is looped around the frame. It was found during excavations at the College of the vicars choral of York Minster at Bedern (a vicar choral sang in the choir as a deputy for a canon of the Minster, and lived in the college with his fellow vicars). The brooch was retrieved from a 13th-century layer close to a residential building, but it seems unlikely that any individual vicar would have had the wealth necessary to purchase such a brooch. It may have belonged to a visitor rather than an inhabitant of the college.

Above: Gold brooch from Bedern, with a gripping hand (diameter 16mm)

Right: Detail of the twisted multi-strand gold wire of the brooch from Bedern

Dress fastenings and fittings of various types are quite commonly recovered archaeological artefacts, found from the time of the Romans onwards. Often made of base metals, they are usually small and appear to have been easily lost. The small decorative metal objects illustrated here are examples of a type of fitting called a 'strap-end'.

The precise function of strap-ends has been the subject of debate for some time, but there seems little doubt that they are in some way associated with clothing. As their name indicates, they may have been attached to the ends of straps or, perhaps more commonly, to the ends of girdles. Girdles of silk or another textile were worn by women in the Anglian (Anglo-Saxon) period. They would encircle the waist, over the gown, and strap-ends would be fitted one to each end of the girdle to prevent it fraying, and perhaps also making it hang down attractively. Some men may also have used strap-ends on their leather belts. Occasionally a strap-end has been found with decoration which appears to match that found on a buckle, as if the two fittings were made as a matching pair.

The two strap-ends illustrated here are both from Anglian levels at Fishergate. Although slightly different in design, they incorporate the typical features of a split end with one or two rivet holes for attachment to the girdle or strap, and decoration at the opposing tip involving some form of animal head. The longer and narrower strap-end appears to have repeatedly used the animal head motif, with a pair of raised ears, eyes and snout at the tip, and behind, two further pairs of ears, eyes and snout, separated by two bands of dots. On the other example, the animal head at the tip is only just recognisable, while the main body of the strap-end is decorated with an incised lattice decoration, inlaid with red enamel.

Copper alloy strap-ends from Fishergate (length of longer example 52mm)

Small dress fittings such as these copper alloy buckles appear to have been frequently lost or discarded over the centuries, judging by the numbers that are recovered in excavations, but it is tempting to speculate that the Anglian (Anglo-Saxon) owners of these two little buckles would have been particularly disappointed at their loss. Both have been well decorated and have been ornamented with silver to make them look even more attractive. The buckle on the left has lost its pin but between the pin hole and the rivet hole for attachment to a strap it has been beautifully decorated with an engraved animal, a crouching beast with its head turned back towards its tail. It has a squarish snout and speckled body, and its outline has been defined by silver inlay. Quite similar in shape, the buckle on the right retains its pin, and also the two rivets for attachment; it has a three-leaf motif below the rivets, and the whole buckle has been silver plated.

Left and Right: Decorated copper alloy buckles, plated with silver (length 30mm and 33mm)

Below: Detail of engraved animal on the buckle shown left

Both these buckles have something in common with another form of strap fitting, the strap-end, and may well have been designed as companion pieces to them. The backward-looking beast and the pendant leaves are both motifs that have appeared on strap-ends of the same period — though not on those illustrated on p.48 — while the pointed tips of both buckles may have been designed to imitate those of strap-ends which typically terminate in an animal head with prominent snout.

The buckles may seem quite small to us and the apertures through which the attached straps would pass are also small. This implies that belts were made of narrow strips, and were probably less substantial than many of those in use today. In fact, at this period, strap-ends are more commonly found than buckles, which occur infrequently before the Norman Conquest, suggesting that they had a less important role as dress fittings than they were to have in the medieval period and today.

It seems evident from surviving busts, statues and paintings of Roman women that they were just as preoccupied with their appearance as any modern woman. Frequently they are depicted with very long hair in elaborate styles, ranging from a bun twisted onto the nape of the neck to very complex curled and layered designs. These all made use of pins to keep the hair in place, so it is not surprising that hairpins, large and straight and often with decorative heads, are common finds on Roman sites. Pins have been found close to or beneath skulls in a number of late Roman female burials, and, in York, the body of an adolescent girl of the 4th century was found complete with hair in a bun secured by two jet pins.

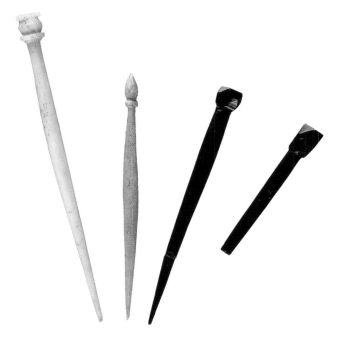

Most pins were made of metal, bone, glass or jet, the most decorative ones tending to be made of metal, although some bone pins have also been found with elaborately decorated heads. The majority of pins of all materials, however, had simply shaped heads, as do the bone and jet examples illustrated here. Most would have been made by craftsmen, and some bone and jet pins have been identified as having been lathe-turned. Some of the bone pins, however, could have been made in the home, being simply formed using a knife. Most jet pins had spherical or faceted heads, but more decoratively shaped heads in the form of a two-handled vase or 'cantharus' (see p.20) have also been found, as in the York burial.

The raw material for the jet pins would have been obtained from the north-east coast around Whitby, but analysis has shown that other jet-like substances were also used, which cannot be distinguished from jet with the naked eye. It is possible that some of the York pins were also made from these materials.

Above: Group of Roman hairpins: at left, two bone pins from 9 Blake Street; at right, two jet pins from 24–30 Tanner Row (length of pin at left 75mm)

Left: A Roman girl's hairpiece secured with two jet pins. Reproduced by kind permission of York Museums Trust (Yorkshire Museum)

Large pins of the Roman period appear to have been used to secure hairstyles (see p.50). Pins of a similar size found in Anglian and Anglo-Scandinavian levels seem to have had a different function, however, as dress fastenings. Often made of copper alloy, and frequently with decorative heads, they have been regularly found on sites in York and elsewhere. Several have been found in graves, near the tops of the bodies, which suggests that they probably secured clothing such as cloaks. The form of the head on the pins varies. Those illustrated here incorporate a ring and are known as ringed pins.

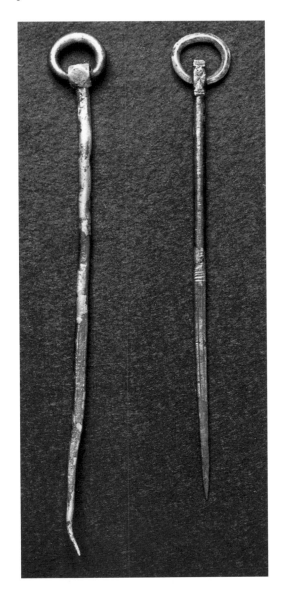

Apart from being faceted, the head of the pin on the left is undecorated, but the other one has simple decorations. It has an incised line design on its head and incised grooves on its shank. Other ringed pins have stamped dots decorating the head. The metals used to make the pins have been analysed. Both ring and pin of the undecorated example are made of brass, while the one with an incised line design has a brass ring but a bronze pin. This suggests that the pin and ring may not have been made together, and that the ring might be a replacement. The ring was probably not simply a decorative element, but may have had a function. Pins have been found with a cord attached to the ring. The cord would probably have looped around the end of the pin in order to secure it in place when it was stuck through clothing.

Ringed pins similar to these, with many variations in head and ring form, have been found in considerable numbers in Ireland, where they probably originated. The Coppergate pins illustrated here date to the 10th century, a time when Dublin and York enjoyed close political and commercial links. These pins may well have arrived in York as a result of trade across the Irish Sea.

Ringed pins from Coppergate (length of pin on the left 180mm)

Silk cap

The site at 16–22 Coppergate produced many fascinating objects, but one of the most exciting finds must be a virtually complete silk headdress, found twisted and crumpled up in a late 10th-century pit. When untangled, the headdress proved to be a simple hood-shaped cap, made from a rectangle of fabric, and clearly repaired at some time with a circular patch. Stitches for the attachment of linen ribbons, used for tying the cap under the chin, were found on the front edge of the hood, although the ribbons themselves had not survived.

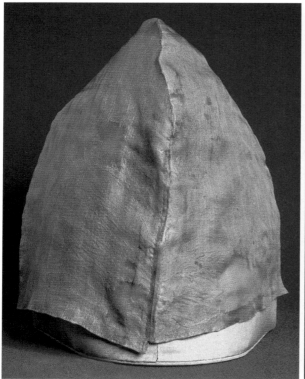 

Top left: Rear view of the silk cap after reconstruction

Top right: Side view after reconstruction

The Coppergate cap is similar to one found in Lincoln, but both appear to be a style of headdress that was previously unknown. Contemporary illustrations of headgear in Anglo-Saxon manuscripts show 'wimple'-type coverings, which completely concealed the neck and head, and framed the face. Anglo-Saxon words for headgear, however, included *hod* or hood and *cuffie* or cap, so such items may have existed. The fact that these caps have been found in the Danelaw area of England, which was under Viking influence, suggests that we should perhaps look for a Scandinavian origin. An 11th-century wall painting in a church in Kiev in Russia depicts four daughters of King Yaroslav, at least one of whom is wearing a hood-like headdress, perhaps a symbol of her unmarried status. Kiev was a Viking-ruled town on the main route from the Baltic to Byzantium, one of the sources of silk. It seems quite possible that silk was being traded along this route, eventually reaching Scandinavia, and ultimately England, where it was distributed within the Danelaw (Yorkshire, East Anglia and the east Midlands).

What brought the cap to Coppergate? Well, apart from the cap, there were many other fragments of silk found on the site, and it seems most likely that the silk arrived there as lengths of fabric in order to be cut up and made into caps and perhaps other items of dress. It has even been suggested that the Lincoln cap is so similar to the one from Coppergate that it too was made in Jorvik. The 10th century at Coppergate was a period when much textile production, involving spinning, dyeing and weaving of various fibres, was being undertaken. Production of exotic silk caps appears to have been another element of this busy scene, presumably supplying the wealthier citizens of Jorvik.

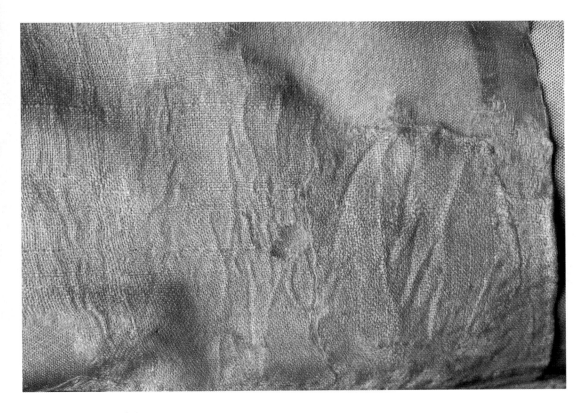

Detail of the silk fabric

Sock

Luckily for us, the damp soil conditions in York have preserved materials that would not normally survive. One object of particular interest is this woollen sock, made in a textile technique known as *nålebinding*.

Nålebinding derives from two Norwegian words — *nål*, meaning needle, and *binding*, meaning to bind. In English it is sometimes referred to as knotless netting, looped needle netting, or single-needle knitting. The technique uses an eyed needle and creates fabric by sewing lengths of thread to form a meshwork of interlocking loops, which does not unravel like knitting or crochet. To make a sock, work starts at the toe with a single loop of yarn and a series of interlocking loops are created in circles from this original loop. Shaping is done by adding extra loops or missing out loops. The result is a thick and stretchy fabric.

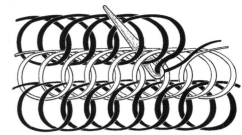

The nålebinding technique used to produce the wool sock

Other objects made using this technique include mittens, hats and bags. Three thick bone needles found at Coppergate could have been used for this type of work, although nothing else made by *nålebinding* has ever been found in England. It seems more likely that the sock found its way to Coppergate on the foot of a Scandinavian settler or trader, perhaps inside a shoe (see p.55-6) which also seems to have come from outside England.

The sock seemed to be badly worn when it was found in the backyard of one of the 10th-century wattle buildings at Coppergate, and it appeared that it might have been patched. It had a narrow red band around the ankle; this had been dyed using the root of the madder plant which provides a dark reddish-purple dye (see p.106). It is unclear whether this band was a decorative edge or whether the sock continued into a red stocking-type garment, the rest of which was lost. If ankle socks like the Coppergate sock were used at this time, they would not have been visible under the shoe, which would explain their absence from illustrations of contemporary costume. Long socks were occasionally represented in late Anglo-Saxon illustrations, including one of the Viking-born King Cnut, but garters or leg-bindings are more typical leg-coverings at this period.

The earliest known examples of *nålebinding* are prehistoric, deriving mainly from Denmark, although there are also some fragments from Switzerland. Post-Roman examples include a sock found in Egypt, some tricoloured fragments, presumed to be from stockings, from Finland, and mittens found in Sweden, Norway and Iceland. More recent examples have been found as far apart as Lapland and South America.

Wool sock after conservation (actual length 250mm)

Over 1,700 leather shoes and shoe fragments, mainly of Anglo-Scandinavian and medieval forms, were recovered from the wet soil at 16–22 Coppergate. Two of the most complete Anglo-Scandinavian shoes are featured here.

Leather shoe made from a single piece of leather (adult size 7 ¹/₂)

The first is a nearly complete shoe for the left foot, and is one of only five shoes found that were made from a single piece of leather. The shoe is cut with a central sole section and the two halves of the uppers (sides and top) to either side. These fold up around the foot and were sewn together to make the complete shoe. A seam runs down the centre of the top of the shoe from the throat (opening for the foot) to the toe, and the shoe was fastened by a drawstring that passed through pairs of slits around the top edge and tied at the front. This shoe style has not been found anywhere else in Britain. As with the woollen sock (see p.54), it may have arrived in York on the foot of a foreign trader or perhaps a slave.

Most Anglo-Scandinavian shoes are of turnshoe construction. In this method of shoemaking, the leather was cut to shape, with separate uppers and sole, the shoe was moulded on a wooden last, and the uppers were stitched to the sole with the shoe inside out. At this point, the shoe was turned right way out — hence the term 'turnshoe'. The second shoe illustrated here was made in this way for a right foot. It is an ankle shoe fastened with a double flap and toggles over the instep; one of the two toggles still survives.

There may not have been as many styles to choose from as today, but fashion seems to have had a part to play even in 10th-century footwear. As with many modern styles, Viking-Age shoes tended to be narrow, often too narrow for the toes. This has the effect of forcing the big toe inwards, which over a period of years can lead to a bunion. Slashes seen in some shoes were probably made to relieve pressure on bunions. Large amounts of leather offcuts were also found at Coppergate, indicating that leather workers must have worked in the area, both making and repairing shoes. One of them may have used a last (a solid foot-shaped model used for shaping shoes) made from alder, which was found in Viking-Age deposits at 6–8 Pavement, less than 100 metres away from Coppergate.

Continued overleaf

Above: An ankle shoe fastened with toggles (reconstructed length 235mm)

Below: Part of a slip-on shoe which has been slashed to relieve the pressure from a bunion

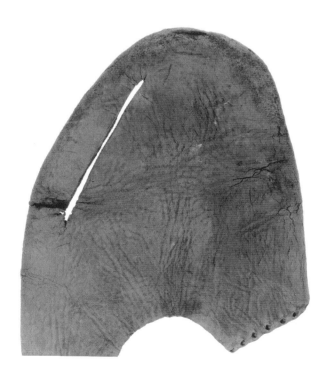

The wonderful range of colours and light found in amber — from light yellows through to deep oranges, from completely transparent to completely opaque — makes it a natural choice for jewellery. Amber is fossilised tree resin, formed millions of years ago, and it was a material much favoured by the Vikings for pendants, beads and amulets. In fact, the world's largest amber deposits are found on the shores of the Baltic Sea, where amber has been harvested, traded and crafted into decorative objects for thousands of years.

The pendants found at Coppergate appear to be one product of craftsmen working amber at the site; other items they produced include rings and beads. We know this because fragments discarded during production have also been recovered. Some of these are unfinished objects, sometimes thrown away because they went wrong or broke during manufacture. Some raw amber was also found, and when this was analysed, it proved to be Baltic amber. This amber can be collected from beaches around eastern England, as it floats across the sea. But the number of amber items and the quantity of waste found at Coppergate suggests that amber was imported from the Baltic region.

The wedge shape of the pendants was made by carving the material with a knife. First of all the size and shape was roughed out, and then the perforation was made. This was drilled through from both sides making an hourglass-shaped hole. The final stages removed the working marks and then the whole object was polished.

Although sometimes worn alone in the Viking period, pendants were also often added to necklaces of glass, metal and crystal beads, making them very colourful and elaborate decorations.

Beads and pendants, both finished and unfinished, made of amber from the Baltic, showing a wide variety of colours and translucence

Gold, pearl and garnet ring

A spectacular gold finger-ring set with precious and semi-precious gems was found at Coppergate, in a pit close to a cobbled path which was being used in the mid 13th century, a time when the wearing of gold rings was becoming popular with those who could afford them. Such a fine ring was clearly the possession of a wealthy individual, and its loss must have been greatly regretted.

Gold finger-ring from Coppergate set with a pearl and four garnets (diameter of pearl 6mm)

The front of the ring is cruciform in shape, set with a central pearl in a raised collet (setting), which appears to be integral with the head; four pink stones, identified as almandine garnets, and set on high collets, are placed at the ends of the arms of the cross.

Analysis of the ring showed that the hoop has a gold content of c.80%, slightly better than 18-carat gold which is 75% pure gold by weight. The shoulders are decorated with a black inlay, which has been identified as niello, an alloy of silver, copper, lead and sulphur which is rubbed into an engraved pattern on silver or gold and then fired. Darkened areas remain in the crevices after the object is polished. Interestingly, the decoration is neither symmetrical nor a mirror image on the two shoulders. On one shoulder the design consists of five chevrons pointing away from the head. On the other shoulder, the design is a zigzag with other lines crossing it at an angle, going round part of the shank as a continuous design. Punched circles, frequently incomplete, are also incorporated in both designs.

Despite being buried for 700 years, the condition of the pearl was remarkable. It was almost undamaged and its orient (mother-of-pearl multi-coloured gleam) was still in evidence. Without dismantling the ring it is impossible to tell whether the pearl is complete, a half pearl or a blister pearl (a pearl which grows attached to the lining of the shell and therefore has a part not covered with mother-of-pearl). Nor is it possible to tell whether the pearl is held purely by the setting, or whether it is part-drilled and held by a peg as in a modern pearl earring. It is probably a freshwater pearl, as marine pearls were not readily available until the late 15th century when the Spanish reached the New World. Possible sources for freshwater pearls at this time may have included Cumberland, Wales and Scotland.

The four garnets are slightly irregular, and are probably small polished pieces of water-worn gem gravel. They are not claw set: the gold on the tops of the collets has been thinned and then rubbed over the margins of the stones. It is possible that the garnet on the shoulder which has the zigzag design is a replacement, or has come out and been reset at some time, as it is set lower than the others, but the colour is a good match.

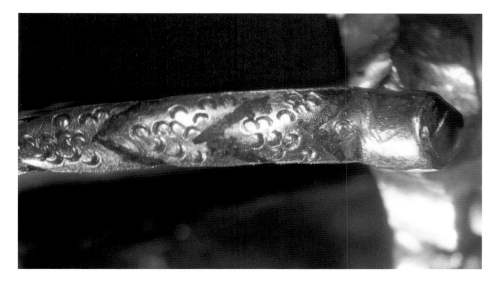

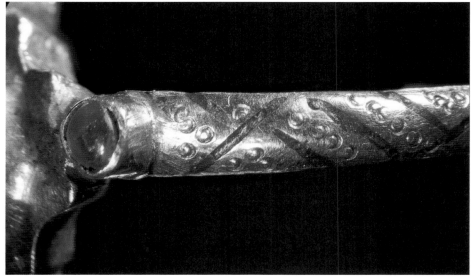

Details of both shoulders of the ring, showing that the decoration is neither symmetrical nor a mirror image

Arm-rings

During the Viking Age precious metals such as gold and silver were treated as bullion and often cast into ingots, to be cut up for use as currency as and when required. Another popular method of storing wealth was as jewellery, which was worn by both sexes. Many Viking silver hoards, buried for safekeeping but not recovered by their owners, consisted of objects such as brooches, arm-rings and finger-rings. Unfortunately, York has not so far produced a Viking-Age silver bullion hoard, but a decorated silver arm-ring was found in a female burial at the church of St Mary Bishophill Junior, in one of four graves belonging to early Scandinavian settlers in the city.

One advantage of storing wealth in the form of jewellery was that it could easily be displayed in order to impress others. Less wealthy people emulated their richer counterparts by wearing jewellery of similar forms, but made of less expensive metals. The arm-ring illustrated here is made of pewter, an alloy of lead and tin, and it appears to have been designed for a young adult, aged about 12–15. It is one of three arm-rings found in 10th-century levels at Coppergate, the others being made of tin and pure lead.

Smaller rings made in a similar fashion to the arm-rings were also found at Coppergate. The simple ring of single-strand copper alloy wire, with the ends twisted around each other, may have been used for a finger-ring, but the knotting of ends is a common feature of Viking rings of various sizes and functions, and rings such as these have also been used on brooches, necklaces, and some types of ringed pin. There is also evidence that they were used as suspension loops for implements such as tweezers (see p.71).

Above: Pewter arm-ring from Coppergate (diameter 46mm)

Right: Copper alloy twisted wire ring from Coppergate (diameter 23mm)

Jet bracelet

This beautiful, highly polished jet object is a Roman bracelet, more specifically a bangle — this is a form of bracelet that is inflexible and solid, as compared to bracelets made up of beads, also used in the Roman period. Bangles could be circular or oval. The oval ones, such as this example, were easier to put on and off because they allowed for the shape of the hand. Circular bangles would have been produced on a lathe, but this shape would have been cut using a knife, starting off with a disc-shaped slab, on which the edge was first smoothed and rounded. Then cuts were made until a ring was removed, and subsequent shaping, such as the terminals or other decoration, would be cut. Although it is thought that this bracelet is made of jet (which could have been obtained from the north-east coast around Whitby), the material has not been analysed, and other similar materials such as shale, which is also black and can be polished, are also known to have been used.

Roman burials excavated in London have revealed that women sometimes wore several bracelets or bangles at once, mainly of copper alloy. They probably reflect a fashion for wearing many bangles (a trend much in evidence again today) rather than representing a conspicuous display of wealth. Some must have been worn to make more than a fashion statement, however. Evidence from London also shows that wealthier women wore silver and rare imported elephant ivory, materials which quite clearly indicated wealth and status. These bangles and bracelets were found in association with female skeletons, but many types of jewellery including brooches, ear-rings and finger-rings, as well as bracelets, are thought to have been worn by both sexes in the Roman period. Expert analysis suggests, however, that jet had a special significance for women, and that jet artefacts and hairpins may be taken to indicate a female burial, even if no body is present. It seems that to the Romans, jet was considered to have mystical properties specifically beneficial to women. According to Pliny in his *Natural History*, the fumes from burning jet were said to relieve certain female complaints!

Above: Jet bracelet from 24–30 Tanner Row (diameter 82mm)

Left: Fragment of a spiral jet bracelet from 24–30 Tanner Row (length 27mm)

Glass beads

Necklaces of colourful beads have been used to decorate the human body at least since the time of the ancient Egyptians. On excavations, beads are often recovered singly, unless they have been buried in the form of a necklace in a grave. Certainly in York they tend to occur individually, although often in great numbers, and they can be made from a variety of materials including stone, glass, bone, shell, jet and amber. Each bead is usually of one colour only, but occasionally polychrome glass beads are recovered, and one of the most spectacular and well-publicised examples is illustrated here.

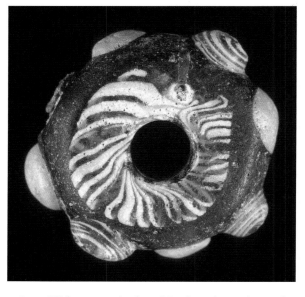

Recovered under the glare of television cameras, this splendid bead was found on a site in Walmgate which was being excavated by Channel 4's *Time Team* when they filmed a live three-day dig in the city in 1999. The main body of the bead is blue, but it has been decorated with eight eyes around its circumference. Four are opaque yellow, and these alternate with more complex bicoloured eyes made from a blue and white twisted glass rod. In addition, a blue and white twisted glass rod was trailed around the perforation on each end. These twisted glass rods are like strings or cables, and sometimes the beads are called string or cable beads. Usually the end twists are left proud, but here they have been marvered or smoothed flat. Although found in the very bottom of a medieval cesspit at Walmgate, the bead in fact dates from the later 7th/8th or 9th century, and was almost certainly made in Ireland.

The other unusual bead illustrated here is made from an emerald, and although found in an Anglian (8th/mid-9th century) deposit at Fishergate, it is more likely to be Roman. In fact, emeralds have been used in jewellery since the Egyptian period, and it is possible that this stone actually came from mines in Egypt. The hexagonal section of the bead makes use of the natural hexagonal crystal form of the stone. After shaping it would have been polished using a fine abrasive such as sand, and the perforation would have been drilled. If this bead dates from the Roman period, and it certainly appears to have been quite worn by the time it was deposited in the ground, it might have been used on a gold necklace strung with a series of such beads, or alternatively as a single stone on a drop ear-ring. It could also have been re-used in the Anglian period before finally being lost. No doubt both owners of these lovely beads would have been very sad to have mislaid them.

Above: Polychrome glass bead from Walmgate (diameter 18mm)

Left: Emerald bead from Fishergate (length 17mm)

Chatelaine

It is not often that archaeologists can state with some certainty that a particular object, or group of objects, belonged to a woman rather than a man. Many items that we might today think of as specific to women, for example brooches or finger-rings set with gems, have in the past been used by both sexes, and care has to be taken not to make assumptions about ancient artefacts on the basis of present day customs. Occasionally, however, it is possible to make such an attribution — this collection of iron objects and fragments, which at first sight seems rather unpromising, is one such case.

All these iron pieces come from the same object, known as a chatelaine (the word means the keeper of a castle, the person entrusted with the keys). Both the pronged implements in the set are keys, while the incomplete stems are probably keys from which the bits have broken off. The surviving keys are of a type which would have been used on locks fixed onto furniture such as chests, or on doors. This particular chatelaine appears to have consisted of two rings, from each of which a number of keys hung; the rings themselves were connected by iron chains. A possible reconstruction shows how it might have looked originally.

What makes us suspect that this belonged to a woman? Well, most chatelaines of this type have been found in graves of the early Anglian (or Anglo-Saxon) period (late 6th or 7th century), and where the sex of the body in the burial could be determined, it has invariably been female. Some chatelaines had other implements attached such as tweezers, or tools for cleaning nails or picking teeth. Most seem to have hung from the waist or hips, presumably from a belt or girdle. This suggests that they were considered worthy of display and may have been worn with pride as a status symbol.

Above: Chatelaine fragments from Fishergate (length of longest key 122mm)

Left: Interpretation of the original design of the chatelaine

To many people, spurs are perhaps most commonly associated with medieval knights and jousting, but, in fact, they are known from as far back as the time of the Romans. Those illustrated here are from the Viking period. At all times, spurs appear to have been rather more than just functional objects, designed to help with horse riding — they were also fashion statements and status symbols.

When first made, both these spurs would certainly have looked splendid. Both have a decoratively shaped projection, called a goad, at the heel, and also decorative incised lines along the spur on one side only, presumably the side that was visible when the spur was being worn. Traces of tin plating have been found on the first — this would have given the decoration a silvery appearance. At the ends, there are terminals with slots. The straps for attaching the spur to the foot would have passed through these, as we can see in the reconstruction drawing. The first spur still retains part of a plate which would have been attached to the strap.

It is known that in the medieval period spurs with gilding on them were specifically destined for use by knights. It seems likely that in the Viking period, too, plated spurs such as those illustrated here were the possession of men of rank and wealth. It seems unlikely that any inhabitant of Coppergate would have worn such a fine accessory, and it is more likely that spurs were being manufactured there. Certainly, there is evidence that other iron objects such as dress fittings were made and plated with tin on the site.

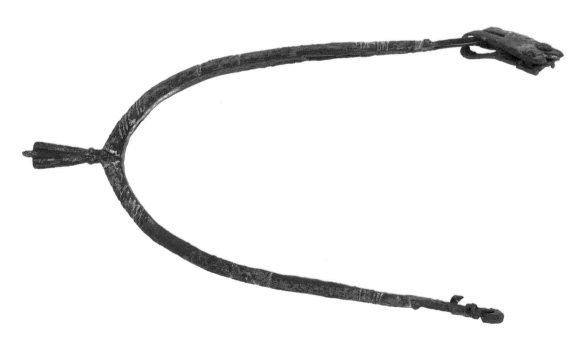

Almost complete tin-plated prick spur (length 133mm)

Above: Another Anglo-Scandinavian prick spur (length 138mm)

Below: Reconstruction drawing showing how a medieval prick spur would have been worn

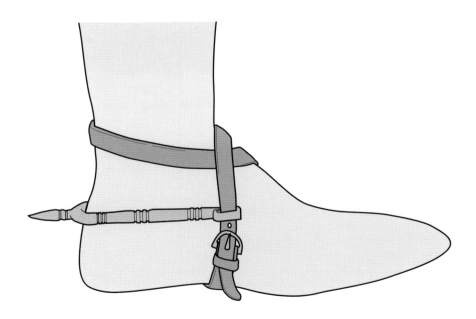

Composite combs

Male fashion icons may seem a very 21st-century phenomenon, but as long ago as the 12th century writers were commenting on the influence exerted by men who appeared to be taking great trouble over their appearance. One such writer was John of Wallingford, commenting about the conduct of Scandinavians in this country. In his opinion, they '... *caused much trouble to the natives of the land; for they were wont, after the fashion of their country, to comb their hair every day, to bathe every Saturday, to change their garments often, and set off their persons by many such frivolous devices. In this matter they laid siege to the virtue of the married woman, and persuaded the daughters even of the noble to be their concubines*'.

Amazing to think that such seemingly innocuous objects as the combs illustrated here could have aroused such passions! Both the combs here are of types used at the time that John was writing, and they have been found in considerable numbers in York. As the photographs show, they take virtually the same form as modern combs, although they differ in terms of the materials used and the method of manufacture. Both are made of antler, a material chosen because of its strength and flexibility. No part of an antler was large enough to construct a one-piece comb, so the combs had to be composite, made up of several parts. This method of manufacture had its advantages, as individual parts could be replaced if they became damaged or broken. The two combs illustrated here differ slightly in that the main body of the comb from Coppergate is composed of a pair of plates, called connecting plates, whereas the comb from High Ousegate makes use of a naturally curving antler tine with a slot cut in. A series of tooth plates have been riveted between the connecting plates, and within the slot. The case shown with the Coppergate comb would have been made to fit a particular comb, though probably not the one illustrated here.

To make the comb, the antler worker would first have to remove the curved ends or tines from the antler, which would have been collected from the wild after it had been shed by the deer. The main body of the antler, or beam, would then be cut into the lengths required for the connecting plates and tooth plates. The beam would be split into quadrants, and the porous inner tissue and rough outer surface was removed from these. The remaining hard compact tissue was shaped into the plates, and then the connecting plates and sometimes the end tooth plates were decorated with patterns of incised lines and stamped dots. Then the tooth plates were riveted in and the teeth were cut. Finally, the tops of the tooth plates were trimmed off so that they lined up with the top of the comb.

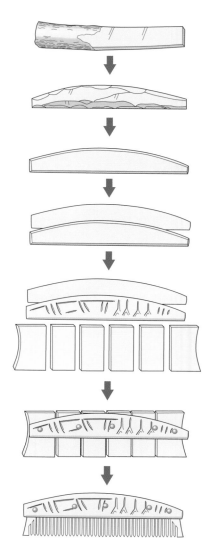

Diagram showing the steps in the manufacture of an antler comb

*Above: Composite comb and comb case from Coppergate, both made of antler
(length of comb 122mm)*

Below: Composite comb from High Ousegate made of antler (length 166mm)

Objects which seem to us in the 21st century to be entirely functional and of no personal value have not always been viewed in this way. As we have seen, combs clearly used to be highly valued, often beautifully decorated and sometimes kept in their own cases. Another example of a personal accessory we would surely consider of little interest is tweezers. The form of these simple implements has barely changed at all since Roman times but, on occasion, they were decorated and personalised, so they were obviously valued possessions. The pair of copper alloy tweezers illustrated on p.71 is from Anglo-Scandinavian deposits at Coppergate. It has a small wire ring attached to the loop at the top of the tweezers, presumably so that it could be hung from a belt or girdle. The ring has a white glass bead threaded on to it as an extra embellishment. The tweezers also have stamped ring-and-dot motifs on the arms.

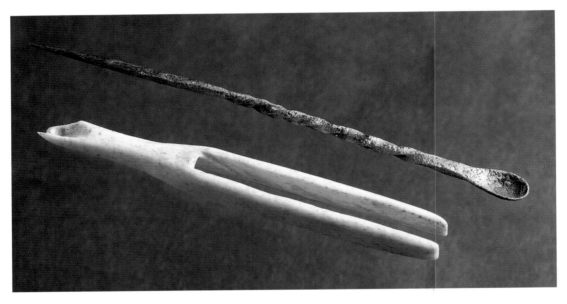

Top, copper alloy ear scoop and tooth pick from Coppergate; Bottom, bone toilet set from Fishergate (there would once have been an ear scoop at the broken end). Length of toilet set 66mm, ear scoop 84mm

Other small accessories for maintaining bodily cleanliness include ear scoops, presumably for removing wax. A medieval bone toilet set from the Gilbertine priory at Fishergate cleverly manages to combine a set of tweezers with an ear scoop, the scooped end unfortunately being damaged. The other metal implement illustrated here combines an ear scoop with a toothpick, the shaft between them having been decoratively twisted. This was found in a medieval deposit at Coppergate.

Although these particular implements post-date the Roman period, very similar artefacts were also used by the Romans, as noted above. Many people have assumed that such objects as tweezers and nail cleaners must have belonged to Roman women, but, perhaps surprisingly, some have turned up on Roman military sites in what are specifically male areas such as turrets. Care thus has to be taken when making assumptions about what type of person used what type of object in the past — assigning object types to particular genders is not at all straightforward!

Above: Copper alloy tweezers from Coppergate with a glass bead on the wire ring (length 41mm)

Below: Victorian bone toothbrush, with bristles missing (length 151mm). The inscription reads 'Pitterton Margaret St Cavendish Sq'. This was excavated on the site of St Leonard's Hospital in 2001

When these fragments of copper alloy plate, full of holes and with traces of leather on them, were spotted next to the leg bones of a skeleton at the Gilbertine priory in Fishergate, no one was quite sure what they were for. The body was an adult male, approximately 45 years of age at death, who had been buried some time in the 13th or 14th century. The plate fragments were recovered from the area of the right knee where they had stained both the tibia and fibula bones. Perhaps they had been fixed to the man's leg, but for what purpose?

Analysis of the skeleton revealed that the individual, who may have been a member of the priory, suffered a painful rupture of the anterior cruciate ligament in his lower right limb. This may have been sustained after a severe fall, but early references to the Gilbertines playing football might suggest an alternative cause. The same injury put the former England player Paul Gascoigne out of the FA cup final in 1991! However caused, the injury would have left our man with a knee out of alignment, a noticeable limp and a chronic knee infection. Analysis of the rest of the skeleton showed that his right shoulder was higher than his left, suggesting that he used a crutch

It is thought that the plates could represent medical intervention, following a practice recommended by Hippocrates over 2,000 years earlier. The knee would have been encased by the two plates which would have been attached with leather straps. This would prevent the joint from further movement, and enable the individual to continue to walk. The copper may also have been employed for its apparent disinfectant property.

How do we know that some Gilbertine monks played football? Well, in 1321, Pope John XXII granted a dispensation to William de Spalding, a canon from Shouldham — another Gilbertine establishment in Norfolk — for accidentally killing a friend. Apparently, 'During a game at ball, as he kicked the ball, a lay friend of his, also called William, ran against him, and wounded himself on a sheathed knife carried by the canon so severely that he died within six days'. Clearly, football was a dangerous game in the 14th century and led to a variety of injuries, some fatal!

Opposite page: Copper alloy medical plate fragments in situ near the right knee of an adult male skeleton from the Fishergate cemetery (scale unit 100mm)

3
Games, Recreation and Literacy

Bone skates

These simple but effective bone skates have fascinated visitors to the Jorvik Viking Centre since it opened. They were found at Coppergate and date from the 10th century. Several dozen such skates have been found in York, including 42 from Coppergate and others from Bedern, Piccadilly and Fishergate. A small skate recovered from Piccadilly may have belonged to a child. Bone skates have been used in Europe from the Iron Age to the 19th century, but the ones from York have all been found in 10th- to 12th-century deposits.

They were used for skating on ice, and often had a hole for attaching the skate to the wearer's leather boot using a thong. A peg with ties attached to the skater's boot could be lodged at the rear, and there might be another hole at the front where a fastening could be made. Hazel and willow pegs have been found in York. The skates were usually made from horse or cattle foot bones with the surface that would have been in contact with the ice or snow roughly cut. In some instances the small degree of flattening shows that the bone was used virtually in its natural state. Sometimes the toe was trimmed to a point, and sometimes part of the leading edge was cut away to give the toe an upswept profile. Both features would have helped the skater to negotiate uneven patches of ice. The skater would have propelled himself along with one or two poles, rather like modern ski poles. It was mainly the wearer's weight that kept the skates in place, and the feet were rarely lifted from the surface of the ice.

The skates could indicate climate change, a perennially interesting topic. Although the River Ouse in York would have flowed along a less constricted course in Viking times than it does today, and would thus have been more sluggish and ready to freeze, the frequency with which these skates have been found in Viking and Norman levels is one of the principal indicators that the climate was slightly colder than today's. On such evidence whole areas of research may be based!

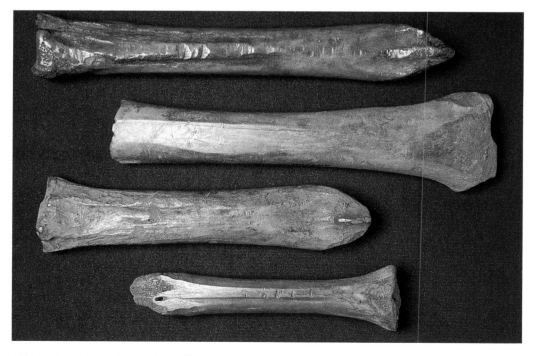

Viking-Age bone skates from Coppergate

Bone skate with a Viking-Age leather boot

Bowling has a long history, with evidence for the game in England traced back to the 13th century. It was, in fact, outlawed by King Edward III in 1365 in order to keep his troops focused on archery practice! The game gradually changed through time. In the 13th century, two small cones were placed at a distance from each other, with the players bowling at them alternately. Later, a small bowl or 'jack' would mark the direction of the bowls. Bowling greens are said to have been invented in England, as used perhaps by Sir Francis Drake on Plymouth Hoe in 1588 whilst the Spanish Armada was approaching. Covered-over bowling alleys were developed during the Middle Ages for noblemen's mansions (among the additions made by Henry VIII to Whitehall were 'divers fair tennice-courtes, bowling-alleys, and a cock-pit'), and for the public. Historian J. Strutt, writing in the 1830s, describes these alleys as 'receptacles of idle and dissolute persons, and the means of promoting a pernicious spirit of gambling among the younger and most unwary part of the community'!

York had its own bowling greens. There was one at Sir Arthur Ingram's house, north of the Minster, newly made in 1634, another in the deanery garden in 1647 and a third at the King's Manor. In 1737 a former bowling alley is mentioned between Bedern and St Andrewgate, measuring 35 yards by 7 yards. This was probably laid out earlier, in the 17th century, when bowls was a popular pastime.

This bowling ball was recovered from 15th-century levels at Copper-gate and is a spindle-turned ash ball. An elongated sphere, it has the con-centric groove tool marks of turning at each end. The ball is almost like a cylinder with rounded ends, so it is unlike the modern bowling ball whose profile has a smooth curve from the tall to the short axis. It has a flatter circumference on which it would have run when bowled, whereas the modern bowling ball runs on a narrower section of the widest part of the circumference. It did not have a deliberately created bias, unlike modern equivalents.

Fifteenth-century spindle-turned bowling ball (diameter 110mm)

Bowling is still popular today in York as elsewhere, continuing a tradition that has persisted for many centuries.

Above: A representation of bowling in the 14th century

Below: Bowling in York today: Osbaldwick v. Selby

Gaming board

Despite the advent of computer games and playstations, board games of a bewildering variety have managed to maintain their popularity today, perhaps because of their essentially social nature. How exciting, then, to unearth ancient playing pieces, dice (see p.82-3) and even part of a Viking-Age gaming board during excavations in York.

Glass, bone, stone and pottery counters have been found on many Roman sites in York. A number of counters have been reworked from glass and pottery by trimming or smoothing broken objects (see p.28-9). The bone and pottery counters found in the silt of the Roman sewers in York may mean that a popular activity in the baths was playing games such as *ludus duodecim scriptorum*, an early form of backgammon, and *ludus latrunculorum*, a form of chess where opposing sets were made of glass of differing colours or with distinguishing marks. The latter, meaning 'the soldiers' game' in Latin, was clearly played by soldiers, and there may be an interesting modern equivalent in 'uckers', a traditional naval game which is an advanced form of ludo (which means 'I play' in Latin). Uckers is still popular today, particularly on submarines where there is little room for other recreational activities.

Viking-Age gaming board from Coppergate with gaming pieces of bone, antler and ivory

Gaming pieces from Viking-Age, Norman and medieval sites have also been found all over the city. Twenty-five pieces of bone, antler and ivory were recovered from Coppergate, including the Viking-Age lathe-turned walrus ivory gaming piece (opposite). It has a hole in its base to fit over a peg on a board. The fine Norman jet chess piece, below (a rook, with the characteristic V-notch cut into the upper surface) was clearly appreciated as it was later pierced for suspension. Other finds include medieval discs of bone or antler, possibly for a game called *tabula* (Latin for 'board' or 'gaming board') which is thought to have been introduced at the time of the Norman conquest. Of course, identification of gaming pieces is not always straightforward. It has been suggested that some of the stone discs may actually have been lids for wooden or ceramic vessels, perhaps indicated by slight wear round the edges due to having been pushed into the neck of some vessel. Archaeology is full of such puzzles!

Norman jet chess piece (length 36mm)

The splendid Viking-Age gaming board shown above, with gaming pieces of bone, antler and ivory, was found in one of the houses at Coppergate. It might have been used there or left there, in pieces, to serve as firewood. This oak example is one section of a board probably comprising five such sections, held together by two raised strips nailed across the ends of the planks. It is marked with intersecting incised lines forming three rows of fifteen squares or rectangles. When complete, the board would have had fifteen rows and probably fifteen columns. It would have been used for the Viking game of *hnefatafl*. This was popular in Scandinavia, and is one of many types of *tafl* (a Germanic word meaning 'table') played across Europe in the first millennium. There are references in Icelandic sagas to a fine walrus ivory board being given to King Harold Fairhair, part of a board was found in the Gokstad Viking ship burial and there have been other finds in Scotland, Ireland and Scandinavia. Clearly then, as now, a good game was enjoyed by all.

Above: Viking-Age walrus ivory gaming piece (diameter 21mm)

Left: Roman counters from Blake Street and Swinegate on a modern gaming board

This reconstruction from the Jorvik Viking Centre shows two children playing hnefatafl. An almost full set of pieces was recovered from the floor of a building excavated in Coppergate. The playing pieces were made from a variety of materials including chalk, jet, walrus ivory, antler and bone

It is always a thrill to find an ancient object with an exact modern counterpart, and these dice provide excellent examples of this. They have been recovered in Coppergate, Fishergate, Bedern and the Museum Gardens, and are variously made of stone, jet, antler, bone and ivory. Some such dice are inlaid with calcium carbonate and some with tin. Most display the ring-and-dot motif.

Bone die (length 10mm)

The conventional numbering system used on dice since the Roman period is still in use today, and has the sum of opposite faces adding up to seven (one opposite six, two opposite five, and three opposite four). Interestingly, there was also an alternative numbering system for dice widely in use in the medieval period, from about the 13th to the 16th century, which had one opposite two, three opposite four, and five opposite six. Examples of both numbering systems have been found in York. Such dice would clearly have been used for games of chance, even among the clergy. The rules of the College of Vicars Choral at Bedern, recorded in the 14th or 15th century, felt it necessary to state that 'games of chess and draughts, betting and gambling and throwing dice, within the limits of the hall, are forbidden under a penalty of 3s.4d.'.

Not all the dice found are of standard size and shape by any means. There is one lozenge-shaped die from Bedern which has the sides showing six and one longer than the other sides. The Vicars Choral rules record that on 20 November 1529, 'John Walkewood, a poor clerk, was accused of entering the house of Henry Litherland, at night, and winning money by false dice. He was ordered to say the seven penitential psalms at Matins, in the middle of the choir, and to walk amongst the boys in the procession'! Perhaps John Walkewood used a loaded die similar to the lozenge-shaped one unearthed in Bedern so many years later!

Norman jet dice from Coppergate (length of larger die 12mm)

Above: Viking-Age walrus ivory and bone dice from York (length of large ivory die 30mm)

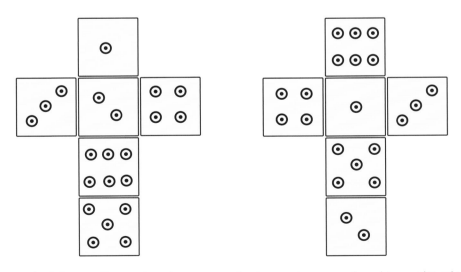

Drawings of all faces, illustrating the two numbering systems employed in medieval times

Writing plays a major part in life today, and writing from the past holds a great fascination for many people. Experts recently placed the writing tablets from the Roman fort at *Vindolanda* in Northumberland as the nation's finest treasure in the British Museum. Writing implements used before the advent of printing range from those used to scratch into wax tablets to others used on beautifully written medieval manuscripts. Many examples of such implements have been found in York.

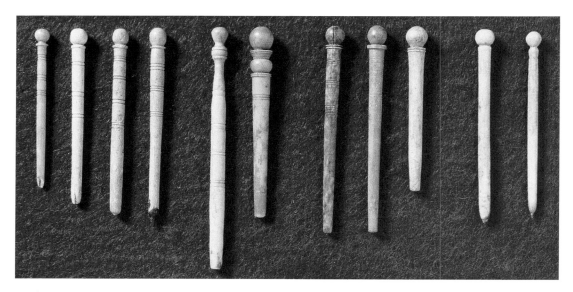

Medieval bone styli from Bedern (length of longest stylus 92mm)

Roman writing was done using a stylus, an implement that made an impression into a waxed wooden tablet or lead sheet tablet. The pointed end of the stylus would make the letters and the blunt end could erase anything not wanted. A number of Roman and medieval styli, made of metal or bone and usually with spherical heads, have been excavated in York. One such would have been used to scribe the wax tablets featured on p.86-7.

Some of these styli with iron tips may in fact be prickers for marking out lines on parchment. Literary activities were very important in monastic life where part of each monk's day was spent copying passages from the scriptures and theological works. Parchment prickers made of bone or iron have been found at several ecclesiastic sites in York, including the Gilbertine Priory of St Andrew. Tiny holes made in vertical lines, probably through several thicknesses of parchment at a time, would mark the position of horizontal lines which could then be marked out.

Lead alloy points were also used during the 12th century. Examples with one pointed and one flattened end have been found on many sites in York, dating from the 11th century to post-medieval times. The functions of the points may differ according to type, and may have been used by craftsmen to make marks on wood as well as being used as pencils in writing or manuscript production.

The lead slate (opposite) has incised lines, irregularly spaced and unruled, on both faces, with the letters 'A' and 'H' clearly visible. The bevelled edges suggest that a wooden frame was originally present. Widespread use of slates in schools appears to date from the late

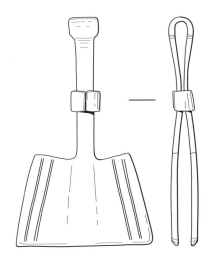

18th century onwards, but this one was found in mid 15th- to early 16th-century levels at Bedern and may be a rare example of a late medieval slate. More recently, children may have used similar slates at the Bedern National School which stood on the site c.1872–1941.

Many other finds in York have been identified as being associated with books, including some interesting medieval book mounts, which had a protective as well as a decorative function, and medieval book clasps for keeping books closed. Such objects can be difficult to identify. Few would probably recognise this small flat object from the 14th century as a page holder to keep documents together or to hold down pages!

Top left: Page holder (width 26mm)

Top right: Reconstruction of a complete page holder

Right: Lead slate (length 130mm)

When eagle-eyed excavation assistant Martin Bartlett spotted a small dark brown object in dark brown waterlogged soil, little could he have known what a treasure he had discovered. Wrapped in a leather cover and of matchbox size, measuring only some 30mm by 50mm and 15mm thick, was a fine set of waxed writing tablets, subsequently dated to c.1350. The leather wrapper was decorated with a tooled design of oak leaves, and the tablets themselves were made of boxwood. Each tablet was about 1.5mm thick and there were eight in total. They turned out to be the smallest and finest set of such tablets to survive in Europe.

One of the 14th-century wax tablets after conservation (dimensions 50 x 30 x 1.5mm)

Seven of the tablets were very firmly attached to each other, with some adhesion of wax from one face to another. Separating the tablets required extraordinary nerve from conservator Sonia O'Connor. Artefact expert Dominic Tweddle has described the decision to go ahead as akin to the gamble taken by hapless contestants on the 'mercifully long dead' game show *Double Your Money,* when the money was a certainty but the box a gamble containing untold wealth or a pair of bicycle clips! In the event, the separation was an enormous success and the contents give us a wonderful glimpse into medieval life.

The first text is written in Middle English and is part of a poem. Not all has yet been deciphered but one phrase has been interpreted as '... still she did not answer me, but she didn't say no...', which suggests that this was a love poem, updated today perhaps to 'She didn't say yes, but she didn't say no'! The second text is some sort of list or set of accounts and the third is part of a legal document, perhaps a letter, written in Latin. It would seem that we had found someone's personal notebook. Whoever it belonged to was literate in both English and Latin, was involved in commercial and legal transactions (maybe as a secretary), and was quite possibly in love! Let's hope that ultimately she said 'yes'!

A replica set of the eight tablets in their leather container

Clay pipes

Clay pipes, dating from the 17th century onwards, are found in considerable numbers in York and throughout the country, demonstrating the widespread popularity of the 'pernicious weed'. Mind you, the growth in the use of tobacco in the early 17th century was encouraged because of its reputed medicinal properties, particularly during plague epidemics. Anyone who has suffered from midges in Scotland may well understand something of the attraction of a smoky, fragrant barrier!

A group of clay pipe pieces from various excavations in York

London was the main centre for early pipe-making, but it seems that the expansion of the industry encouraged makers to move to the provinces from the 1640s. Tobacco-growing too was widespread at this time because of increased demand and high duties on imported tobacco. In fact, in 1677 the Surveyor General of Customs had orders to stamp out tobacco-growing in certain regions, including York. Tobacco shops were first licensed in 1632, and pipe-making began in York. One pipe-maker, John Wright, is recorded as having taken on a poor boy as an apprentice in the city. The familiar tobacconist's shop sign may still be seen today in Petergate in York.

The clay used to make clay tobacco pipes such as these was first washed to remove dirt and then dried and matured on boards. Then it would be beaten with an iron bar to remove air bubbles (called 'blunging') until it was putty-like. Balls of clay were rolled by hand and then into the rough shape to be moulded. A piercing rod passed through the shank of a roll and this was placed in a two-piece mould (made of brass in the early period and later of iron). The assembled mould was pressed in a gin press and the piercing rod was removed. The completed pipes were then dried, trimmed and fired. After firing the mouthpieces were coated with lacquer or wax to prevent the smoker's lips from sticking to the clay.

Such work was financially unrewarding, and early pipe-makers seem to have lived and worked in poorer areas, with small kilns tucked away in the corner of their yards. Nonetheless, their work was prolific, with examples such as these extant some two or three hundred years after their production.

Right: Tobacconist's shop sign in York showing the typical black boy with tobacco leaf headdress and kilt, popular in the 18th century

Below: Two views of a fine clay pipe from 12 Minster Yard decorated on one side with a full-rigged sailing ship and on the other with flowers and foliage (height of bowl 41mm)

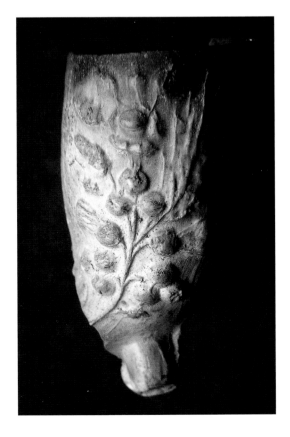

Pan pipes

It is a very rare treat when something as intangible as a one thousand-year-old sound is recovered from an excavation. This is what has happened as the result of a discovery from a 10th-century pit at Coppergate. Amongst the debris in the pit was a small rectangular wooden object less than 10cm long. There was a hole in one corner and five tubes of different lengths had been bored through the wood, the smallest one broken off along the side. What was this strange object? The wood species was identified as box (*Buxus buxus*) and the object was finally revealed as an incomplete wooden syrinx, or pan pipes. Amazingly the notes top A to top E could still be played on it.

The pan pipes found at Coppergate (length 97mm)

The pipes had been very carefully produced. The boxwood plank was bored with a sharp-ended tool called an auger to produce the five parallel-sided tubes of different lengths. Boxwood timber of this size is unusual in Britain as it grows very slowly: this piece was from a tree which was 100–200 years old. This fact, together with the skill required to produce the instrument, meant that it would have been an expensive and treasured possession. The accuracy of the size, depth and separation of the tubes would have been vital to ensure that the notes played true. The hole in one corner would allow the pan pipes to be attached to a belt with a thong.

Had the pipes been broken before they were dumped in the rubbish pit a thousand years ago? Were they dropped, damaged and then discarded? Whatever small disaster occurred, we can only sympathise with the musician who must have believed the instrument had sounded across the roofs and buildings of Jorvik for the last time. How amazed he would be to find he was wrong!

Right: Richard Hall, excavator of Jorvik, plays the pan pipes

Below: Wooden pan pipes with a lyre bridge, bone whistle and tuning peg (see p.95). All these are from Viking-Age York

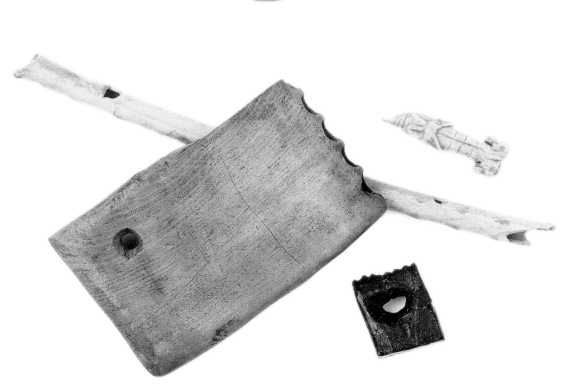

Jew's harp

The Jew's harp is an ancient folk musical instrument, indigenous to south-east Asia and introduced into Europe by the time of the Crusades. It is the only type of medieval percussion instrument to have survived. The name Jew's harp is misleading as the instrument has no Jewish tradition and is not a harp! The alternative name of 'Jaw's harp' is perhaps more appropriate as it is played in the mouth, although it has been suggested that the name is a mistranslation of the French word *jouer*, meaning 'to play'.

This example is from the site of the College of Vicars Choral in Bedern. There is a clear musical association here, as the vicars choral sang services at York Minster in place of the canons who were occupied elsewhere. This instrument has iron arms of the characteristic diamond-shaped cross-section, and a steel tongue set into a small recess at the head. It is about 5cm long. Jews' harps of this form known elsewhere appear to date from the 13th to the 16th century. Most are in a poor state of preservation, and few retain more than part of the tongue. They vary in shape, size and decoration.

The instrument is held in one hand and the frame is lightly supported by the player's teeth. The metal prong is flicked with the fingers of the other hand, and the mouth cavity acts as a resonator. The sound produced is a buzzing note, the tone of which is modified according to the position of the lips, tongue and cheeks.

Jew's harp unearthed in Bedern (length 57mm). The corrosion visible cannot be removed as the object is too fragile

The Jew's harp was principally an instrument of the people, being cheap, uncomplicated and easy to transport. In the late 18th and early 19th centuries the instrument became fashionable, and virtuoso players such as Franz Koch and Karl Eulenstein apparently delighted patrons with their sweet playing, even managing to play more than one instrument at once! The German Dr Mesmer used the instrument to 'mesmerise' his patients, and in Austria in the early 19th century silver Jews' harps were reportedly banned as they were felt to be instruments of seduction! Who knows for what purpose the Bedern instrument was played!

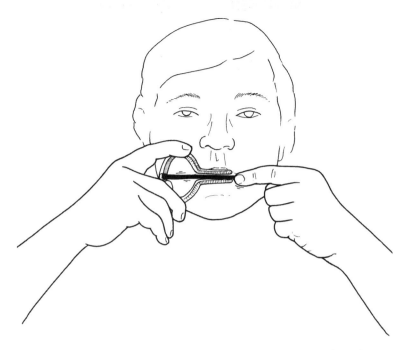

Above: Drawing to show how the Jew's harp is played

Below: Modern Jew's harp, very similar in form to the medieval example

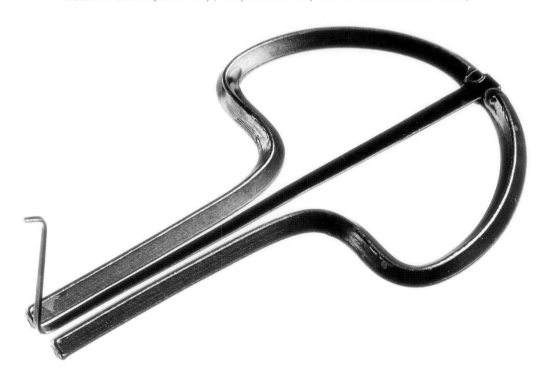

Music plays an important part in the life of York Minster today. The Minster School provides the choristers for evensong and other services, and concerts are a regular feature throughout the year. Music was similarly important to the Minster in medieval times. Vicars choral from the College in Bedern would often be heard singing the services. How appropriate, then, that of all the tuning pegs excavated in York the largest number, twelve, should come from the site of the College of Vicars Choral itself, with the rest coming from other ecclesiastical sites.

Tuning pegs from
Bedern and Aldwark
(length of top peg
63mm)

The tuning pegs date from the mid–late 14th century. All except one are made of bone (the exception is made of antler). They would have been used to tune stringed instruments such as harps, lyres or fiddles by gently turning the peg which would be attached to a string (see reconstruction).

The pegs are all basically the same type, with a squared head, a shaft of circular or sub-circular section, and a drilled perforation at the lower end through which the string passed. They were made by hand rather than by lathe-turning, and file marks can still be seen on some of them. A key would have fitted over the squared end to turn the peg, although one broader-headed peg found in Bedern may have been turned by hand. The differing shaft diameters (4–7mm) and lengths (48–63mm) may indicate that the pegs were made for several different instruments. Some of the pegs are broken at the perforation, an obvious weak point subject to the greatest stress from the pull of the string. Others seem to have replacement perforations, perhaps following a break.

Coppergate provided what has been identified as a 10th- or 11th-century bone tuning key. For it to have functioned as a tuning key its base, now missing, would have had to be cut with a square socket to fit over the head of a tuning peg, as described above. The lack of this base means that its identification as a tuning key is not certain. The object features a

terminal of two birds' heads carved back to back. The elongated 'necks' of the birds are swallowed up by the single mouth of two opposed dragonesque heads which have well-marked ears and ring-and-dot eyes. The opposed heads would provide a grip appropriate for a tuning key.

The object is undoubtedly very fine. Artefact expert Dominic Tweddle has described it as 'a high quality object, not only in workmanship, but in the subtlety of design which plays both with the pairing of animals and changes in plane so that the design can be read from both sides and the eye is naturally carried around the piece. In other words the piece is a fully three-dimensional work, something comparatively rare in pre-Conquest art where objects are usually viewed as a single plane, or a series of disconnected planes'.

Reconstruction showing peg in harp

Two views of 10th- or 11th-century carved tuning key (length 43mm)

Buzz bones

Strange objects, these! With some 90 representatives, they formed one of the most numerous categories of bone objects from the famous 'Viking Dig' at Coppergate, and they have also been found in many other locations in York. The bones used were the trotter bones of pigs, and most have a single transverse hole cut with a knife through the centre of the shaft. The majority are from the late Viking period, but they are present in medieval layers too.

What were they used for? These toggles or 'buzz bones' were once thought to be dress fasteners or bobbins, but they show neither the wear nor polish expected from such uses. It is now thought that they were toys or primitive musical instruments which were made to spin and purr by means of a twine threaded through the hole, stretched between the hands and twisted, and then wound and unwound at speed. Examples of identical bones being used in just this way have, in fact, been recorded in 20th-century Scandinavia and eastern Europe. It seems that they were regarded as ephemeral objects as few have been broken as a result of stress, suggesting that they may have been used just a few times before being discarded.

Above: Buzz bone from Coppergate

Below: Diagram showing a buzz bone in use

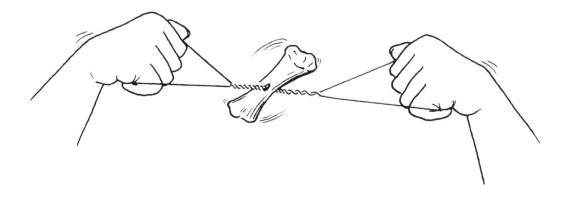

The year 2002 marked Queen Elizabeth II's Golden Jubilee, and celebrations inevitably included the production of many keepsakes and souvenirs. Such commemorative souvenirs have been a popular way of marking royal events since the 17th century, with the earliest known English commemorative material dating from the Restoration of Charles II as king in 1660. New manufacturing methods subsequently led to a boom in production and made such items affordable for the general public.

YAT trainee excavators were reminded that this is a well-established custom in 2001 while digging at the site of the medieval Hospital of St Leonard in York. The Yorkshire Philosophical Society had acquired the site, now in the Museum Gardens, in the 1820s and subsequently constructed a Victorian archaeological garden there. This landscaped garden re-used some of the stonework from the medieval hospital to form decorative features and walls. These were uncovered during excavations, together with objects which had been incorporated into the garden soil.

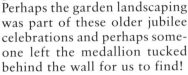

One of these objects turned out to be a copper alloy medallion produced to commemorate an earlier Golden Jubilee, that of Queen Victoria in 1887. The medallion gives the date of Victoria's birth (1819), coronation (1837), marriage (1840) and Golden Jubilee (1887). It also incorporates the rose, thistle and shamrock motifs (with apologies, no doubt, to the Welsh).

Perhaps the garden landscaping was part of these older jubilee celebrations and perhaps someone left the medallion tucked behind the wall for us to find!

Above: Medallion celebrating Queen Victoria's Golden Jubilee (length 37mm)

Left: Trainees excavating the Victorian archaeological garden at the Museum Gardens where the medallion was found. The stone feature shown is a medieval column base

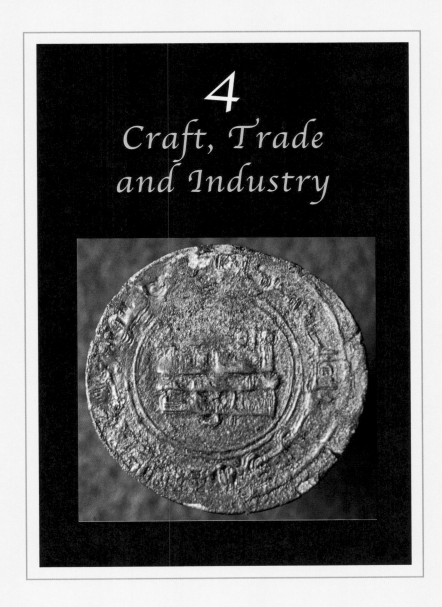

4
Craft, Trade
and Industry

This object is only 38mm in diameter and depicts a slightly stooping figure wearing a long-sleeved knee-length garment with skirt and belt. His right arm is outstretched and the hand holds a purse. Above the purse, and apparently falling into it, are three circles with dots in the centre depicting coins.

What we have is a fine seal matrix made of ivory, probably walrus. It would have been pressed into soft wax to leave an impression to authenticate a document. Royalty, churchmen and nobles all used their own seals to sanction many important charters and laws. This particular one was probably used in day-to-day transactions.

The inscription around the edge of this seal is in lettering known as Lombardic capitals which has been deciphered as reading: '+SIGI . SNARRI. THEOLENARII.'. This translates as 'the seal of Snarrus the toll collector'. The figure in the centre immediately makes sense — here is Snarrus himself collecting a toll payment in his purse. The disc has a little projection at the top which is pierced for suspension and Snarrus might have worn this seal round his neck for safekeeping. The form of the clothing and the lettering suggest that the object dates to the mid 12th century.

Early 12th-century ivory seal matrix showing Snarrus the toll collector (diameter 38mm)

The name on the seal is interesting. It is thought to be a Latinised form of the Scandinavian name Snare or Snorri which is known both as a forename and a nickname meaning 'shrewd' — a useful attribute for a toll collector! The name appears in York and Yorkshire from the time of *Domesday Book* (1086) onwards and there are still Snarrs living in York today. Perhaps they can trace their origins back to this collector of tolls who, in turn, might be a descendant of a Scandinavian settler.

Other seal matrices have been found on medieval sites in York. One from Fishergate, made of copper alloy and depicting a hawk or falcon poised on a hand, appears to have been deliberately cut into two pieces. Seals were personal objects, and perhaps this one was cut up when the seal was no longer to be used, maybe because the owner had died, just as today we would cut up our unwanted credit cards in order to prevent anyone else using them. Nothing much changes!

Medieval seal matrix from Fishergate deliberately cut in two (diameter 28mm)

Detail from the St William window in York Minster showing seals in use (reproduced by kind permission of the Dean and Chapter of York, © Dean and Chapter of York)

The term 'motif pieces' has been coined to describe a variety of fragments of bone and other materials carved in a generally random manner and sometimes with fields of ornamental patterns. Craftsmen used them to work up designs or to perfect their design skills.

Detail showing doglike animals and interlaced plait

Two fine 10th-century bone motif pieces were recovered from Coppergate. The first, 10cm in length, is a bone incised with doglike animals with pinched triangular hips and vigorous actions. This is typical of the classic 9th- and 10th-century Trewhiddle style, named after a Cornish hoard. It is unusual to see quite such free-flowing animals, which suggests that the artist may just have been mastering this style of animal.

The second motif piece is a fragment of a cow's rib, decorated in the Viking Jellinge style which is characterised by ribbon-like interlaced animals with gaping jaws and two-clawed feet. The craftsman first roughed out the design with lightly incised lines before deepening and widening them, all with a knife. Five successive attempts have been made on the bone to construct a particularly intricate piece of animal interlace, and it is possible to work out the order in which the craftsman worked from overlying cuts and the improving design. It has been suggested that the persistent poor drawing of the left-hand side of the designs where the head is far too small may suggest that the workman was strongly right-handed. The intricacy of the pattern probably explains why it was necessary to practise it so many times!

Above: Tenth-century bone motif piece (maximum length 98mm)

Below: Front and back of the 10th-century cow's rib motif piece (length 182mm)

Textile work

York was one of the earliest English towns to establish a reputation as a weaving centre. Wool and flax, dyestuffs and a wide range of textile implements have been found in abundance during excavations, the bulk dating from the 9th to the 15th century. Textile working seems to have been carried out in large part by women, and has even infiltrated the language — spinster is said to derive from 'one who spins' and wife 'one who weaves'!

Iron pieces of wool-comb and probable binding sheet to which teeth would have been attached (see reconstruction opposite top)

The basic raw material for textile production was wool and flax which was spun into yarn. Wool would have come from local sheep, and would have been washed and then combed with a large iron comb-like tool to remove short fibres and align the long fibres parallel to each other. The iron wool-comb teeth illustrated here are from the Viking period and still had wool fibres around the base of the teeth when excavated. Such combs appear to have been used in pairs.

Linen is made from flax, which is a small blue flowering plant of the hemp family. The linen fibres lie between the woody core and outer bark, and had to undergo a complicated series of processes to separate fibre from plant. These included 'rippling' to remove the seeds with a rippler or comb like this 15th-century pine example (perhaps imported from Norway as pine was not grown in England at that time), retting (soaking in water), pounding to break up the flax stems, and scutching, which involved striking the flax to remove stalks and bark. The rare survival of tools in York for all these

Combing wool with a comb in either hand

104

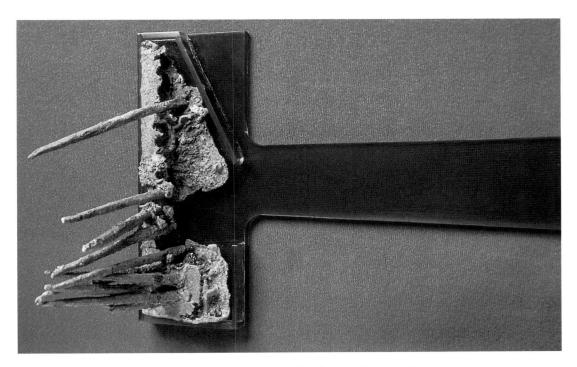

Reconstruction of a Viking-Age wool-comb (length of comb-head 105mm)

processes shows that flax processing was being carried out in the city from at least the 10th century onwards.

When both wool and flax had been prepared, they would have been spun, often using a suspended-spindle, as shown in the diagram on p.106. A length of fibre would be drawn by hand or from a distaff, a stick for holding prepared bundles of flax or wool, and hitched at the top of the spindle, a rod of wood or occasionally bone. It was weighted at the bottom with a 'whorl' which kept the spindle vertical and gave it momentum. Spindle whorls of stone, clay, bone and lead alloy are very common artefacts on Anglo-Saxon, Viking and medieval sites.

After spinning, the yarn could be dyed using natural dyes. Madder, from the roots of the madder plant, produced a warm brick red colour. Madder dye appeared and disappeared with the Romans, but was being

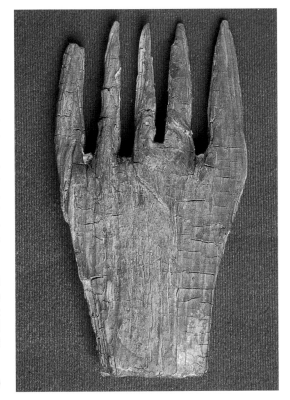

Fifteenth-century flax rippler (length 142mm)

used again in Britain by the 7th or 8th century and was cultivated here by the 10th century. Purple came from lichens, which were probably imported. Woad was used for blue dye. Weld and greenweed, common wayside plants in Britain, gave a yellow colour.

The yarn would then be woven into cloth on a loom. The warp-weighted loom illustrated on p.107 consists of two uprights joined together by a lower cross-beam. The warp threads hung down, weighted by rows of clay loom weights. The two layers of warp threads were held apart by a shaft which could be moved to and fro to allow the weft (the horizontal thread) to pass. A single shaft makes a weave known as 'tabby' and the use of several shafts could make complicated 'twills' and 'herringbone' patterns.

Wool fabric could then be thickened by the use of teasels, which have been identified in Coppergate. These would have been rubbed over the surface of the fabric to draw up the fibres. Cloth could also be ironed with a glass or stone smoother (see p.21).

Wool fabrics show some change in technique through time. In the early 12th century there seems to have been a change towards fewer weaves. The coarse wools common in the Viking Age are rarely present in later textiles, and the cloth is far softer. The deliberate matting of later wool fabrics caused the fibres to felt together and made the more complicated weaves redundant. Medieval linen remains are indistinguishable from Viking ones. Linen weaving continued in York until the 16th century, well after weaving of wool cloth had gone into decline under competition from the West Riding.

The industry had become regulated by the 12th century, and by the late 14th century a division of labour had evolved with no fewer than fourteen different trades. How much fabric was produced for barter or sale and how much for personal use before regulation in the 12th century is unclear. Home production was certainly important, and has given us the term 'homespun' which even today means anything that is made at home or by oneself.

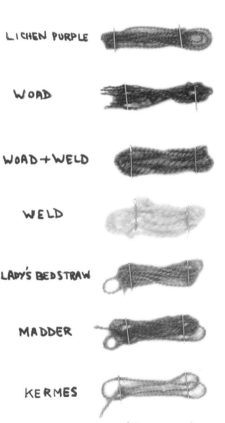

LICHEN PURPLE

WOAD

WOAD + WELD

WELD

LADY'S BEDSTRAW

MADDER

KERMES

OAK GALLS

Above: Spinning with spindle and whorl

Left: Textile dye colours

Opposite page:
Top: Weaving with a warp-weighted loom

Bottom: Examples of textiles from 16–22 Coppergate, including wool fibres, wool yarn, wool textile and silk

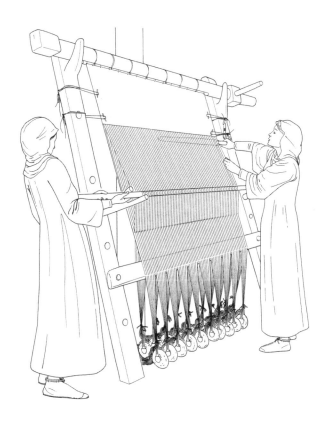

Nowadays we expect the making and distribution of coins to be surrounded by high security. What a puzzle, then, to discover objects associated with coin minting from the floors of two simple 10th-century post-and-wattle buildings in York. The buildings were occupied by metalworkers making everyday objects, including jewellery and dress accessories, from iron, silver, lead, tin and copper. Amongst the debris from this production were two coin dies and some lead trial pieces of mid 10th-century date.

Coin die for St Peter's penny, showing sword (diameter 28mm)

The head of the coin die found in York is extremely interesting as it contains both Christian and pagan symbolism. It is incised in reverse 'St Peter's money', but also displays a Viking sword and Thor's hammer. Such coin dies were used in pairs to produce the impressions on both sides of coins. A metal disc was placed on the bottom die, and the upper die was positioned over it and hit with a hammer to make the coin. The lead strip found is thought to have been a trial piece. However, it has a larger area of metal than is necessary for its impressions, and it may have been used subsequently in mint administration or for the control of authorised dies in use, perhaps as an official record piece. It has recently been suggested that these lead objects with die impressions may have been used as customs receipts for imported goods. The impressions are of the front and back of a penny of King Eadwig of England (955–9).

Were these simple post-and-wattle houses really mints? Did metalworkers produce coins alongside copper brooches and iron nails? Or did they produce only the dies and not the coins themselves? One of the dies is damaged and the other is well worn so perhaps they had been gathered together with other scrap metal for recycling. The debate goes on!

Detail of lead trial piece from Eadwig's reign (153 x 44mm)

Continued overleaf

Above: Viking-Age coin dies and lead trial piece

Below: Striking replica coins at the Jorvik Viking Centre

Samarkand coin

Coins are not unusual finds on archaeological excavations, but this one, with an Arabic inscription, is certainly interesting. The inscription records that it was minted for the Arab caliph (ruler) Isma'il ibn Ahmad at Samarkand, now in Uzbekistan, in the early 10th century. Some sharp practice seems to have been going on as it is made from a copper core covered with tin to imitate a silver coin. The coin, called a dirham, is a contemporary forgery, but is thought likely to have originated in Samarkand and then to have travelled over three thousand miles via the Russian rivers and Scandinavia — where, amazingly, tens of thousands of Arab coins have been found — and on to York. Quite a journey! It may be related to a hoard of Eastern dirhams found in 1859 at Goldsborough, fourteen miles west of York. Sixteen of those were of Isma'il ibn Ahmad, several from Samarkand from precisely the same period.

Tenth-century coin forged in Samarkand and transported to York (diameter 29mm)

Sugar mould

York has long been known as a city with a sweet tooth. Three internationally known sweet manufacturers — Terry's, Craven's and Rowntree's — have all operated in York since the 19th century. The familiar aroma of processing sugar from the British Sugar works often lingers over the city today. How very appropriate, then, that hundreds of pieces of 17th-century red earthenware pottery excavated in Skeldergate should turn out to be from sugar moulds and sugar-refining jars — enough for 132 moulds and 65 jars!

The sherds (pieces of pottery) were unglazed with a smooth white-slipped finish to the interior which would presumably have facilitated the removal of the finished sugarloaf. The moulds are conical in shape, with a hole pierced in the base. The sugar cane would have been chopped and the extracted juices would have been boiled and clarified with lime and bull's blood or egg white before being put into the moulds and stirred. After crystallisation, the moulds would have been placed in jars to allow the excess molasses to drain through. Three sizes of mould and two sizes of jar were found in York, and it seems likely that they would have been used for three qualities of refined sugar, the smallest size yielding the finest sugar.

Subsequent research revealed that there had indeed been a sugar-refiner named John Taylor who had leased a property in Skeldergate for 19 years until his death in 1709. A rather neat tying up of archaeological and historical evidence!

Sugar cane itself seems to have originated in New Guinea, and was well established in India when Alexander the Great's army discovered 'a reed which makes honey without bees'. At that time the sugar was extracted from the cane by chewing and sucking. 'The Persian reed' was subsequently brought to Sicily and Spain and carried by Columbus to the Caribbean. Sugar in Britain was a luxury item and rare before the late 13th century. Sugar cane was imported into Britain from Morocco, and from the mid-17th century from the Caribbean.

Sugar-cone moulds and jars similar to the York ones have been found in London, Southampton, Exeter and Bristol. In the mid 18th century sugar was discovered in the juice of beets, and it is this that is used in the refinery in York today, thus continuing a tradition that had begun some three hundred years ago.

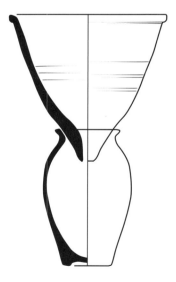

Diagram showing sugar moulds placed in jars to allow the excess molasses to drain through

Sugarloaf with mould fragments found in Skeldergate

Bones from skinning

Archaeological sites often produce huge quantities of bone which can tell us an enormous amount about the past environment and diet. Some of the findings can be extremely interesting and require considerable detective work to make sense of them. One such example is the evidence for skinning of animals in the medieval period.

When excavators sieved 14th-century remains from the site of the College of Vicars Choral in Bedern, they found a huge number of red squirrel bones. Squirrels sometimes appear in medieval art, often as women's pets. An interesting 14th-century copper alloy seal from Bedern actually features a squirrel with its tail curled up over its back, with an inscription running round it reading 'I CRAKE NOTIS (NUTIS?)'; that is, 'I crack nuts'. A bawdy meaning could be read into this inscription, although it could simply be that cracking nuts was an analogy for cracking open a seal.

The red squirrel is Britain's only native squirrel, but now, following the introduction of the larger grey squirrel from North America in 1876, it has virtually disappeared from England, Wales and southern Scotland. To find red squirrel bones in York was thus of some interest in itself. When the bones were analysed, though, it was found that they were, intriguingly, almost all foot bones. The most likely explanation for this is that the feet were brought to the site whilst still attached to semi-prepared pelts (undressed skins). The presence of a knife cut on one of the bones supports this interpretation. Perhaps the finished product was used as fur-edging on the vicars' clerical gowns!

Another example of skinning is provided by the cat mandible (lower jawbone) illustrated here. It is from a cesspit, again from Bedern, which was dominated by cat bones. This bone is 16th- or early 17th-century in date and the parallel knife cuts visible have also been interpreted as the result of skinning for fur.

Above: Drawing of impression of squirrel seal matrix from Bedern (diameter 12mm)

Below: Knife cut marks on a cat mandible resulting from skinning

A second rare species, the pine marten, has furnished us with even earlier evidence for skinning. Excavators digging on the site of a glass factory in Fishergate came across sixteen bones of the pine marten, from 8th- to 9th-century deposits. These are the first records of this species in York. Once again, all of the specimens were foot bones, and one example had fine knife cuts, as illustrated. It seems that here too the bones were derived from skins which came to the site as pelts with feet still attached. Coniferous woodland found in the valleys of the North York Moors seems to be the closest likely source of habitat for these pine martens, although it is possible that there were patches of pine woodland closer to York in the 8th or 9th century. Most furs would have been imported from Scandinavia and the Baltic from an early date, but the presence of feet from animals such as these that would have lived in the York hinterland perhaps suggests that these particular animals were trapped and skinned locally.

Right: Knife cut marks on a pine marten bone
indicative of skinning (length 19mm)

Below: Red squirrel
(photograph © Allan Potts FRPS)

Cowrie shell

An exotic find this, a cowrie shell of the species *Cypraea pantherina*. It provides evidence for the amazingly wide-ranging trade of the Vikings, for it is a species that lives only in the Red Sea. The Red Sea had links with the Viking world via the Caspian Sea or Black Sea. By the 10th century York was second only to London in wealth and population, and exotic goods were imported along trade routes reaching beyond Byzantium (now Istanbul) in the east, Scandinavia to the north and Ireland to the west. Wine and lava quern stones were shipped from northern Europe, and items such as furs, dyestuffs, amber, and soapstone cooking vessels came from Scandinavia. Silks travelled along trade routes from the Middle East and China.

Was this cowrie shell a trade good or a personal possession — a charm or a souvenir? Cowrie shells from Anglo-Saxon England are thought to have served as fertility charms because they mainly occur in female burials, often in containers placed at the waist or feet and sometimes together with other amulets. This shell is a small object, but one which clearly demonstrates contact between York and the Near East. It is interesting to speculate what other exotic but perishable goods such as oils, spices and perfumes may also have been traded in York at this time.

Cowrie shell from the Red Sea found in 10th-century levels in York (length 63mm)

Tools

Many tools have remained virtually unaltered in design since Roman times. Most were made of iron and/or wood, and could be repaired and sharpened on the premises where they were being used. A large number of tools have been unearthed in York for activities including metal working, wood working, leather working, textile working (see p.104-7) and agriculture. These date as far back as prehistoric times with this probable Bronze-Age flint 'thumb' scraper, for example, found in Victorian backfill in the Museum Gardens.

Viking-Age and medieval metal working tools found in York include an anvil, hammer heads, punches, chisels and files. The Viking-Age iron shears illustrated would have been used for cutting iron or a non-ferrous metal plate. The backs of the blades are convex and the cutting edges are bevelled and slightly concave. The handles curve in slightly and have looped terminals.

Right: Possible Bronze-Age 'thumb' scraper

Below: Viking-Age shears or clippers (length 204mm)

Continued overleaf

Wood working tools in York in Anglo-Scandinavian and medieval times include this beautiful Viking-Age mallet which has a willow head and hazel handle. Its circular ends are compressed and burred from use. Such wooden mallets were used for general-purpose wood working, and for any task involving striking a wooden object repeatedly where a metal hammer would damage the wood (such as driving posts into the ground, wedges into a split or pegs into holes).

Other types of wood working tools were made of iron, such as the spoon bit, draw-knife, chisel and axe illustrated here. The axe is a heavy wedged-shaped piece of forged iron with a hole where the wooden shaft or handle was inserted. The axe has changed little in form from Roman times to the present; it could have been used for felling small trees or cutting firewood.

The Viking-Age chisel would have been used for tasks including shaping and cutting designs into wood, or splitting wood. The spoon bit or auger was used for drilling holes in wood. Its form too has changed very little from the 5th century. This one has straight sides, a wedged-shaped tang (the metal projection that goes into the handle) and a rounded point. It is spoon-shaped in cross-section. The handles rarely survive on early spoon bits, but they were probably winged and fitted transversely on to the tang as shown in this reconstruction. The bit cut when rotated. Such spoon bits varied in size according to the diameter of hole required, and would have been used to make many of the wooden artefacts found in York including musical instruments, rake heads and stool seats.

The Viking-Age draw-knife or shave was used to smooth and shave curved objects such as the jointed edges of staves on the inside of circular stave-built vessels like buckets and barrels. The worker would pull the tool towards him along the grain of the wood. This one has a flat blade with tangs at both ends for wooden handles or a single handle between the tangs. Such shaves are known from the Roman period and even today form part of the traditional carpenter's or cooper's tool kit.

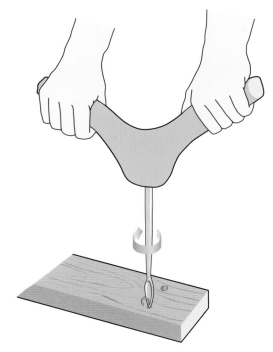

Above: Viking-Age mallet (length of head 120mm)

Right: Reconstruction of a spoon bit in use

Opposite page: Wood working tools: spoon bit, draw-knife, chisel and axe (length of axe blade 152mm). All these objects are made of iron, but the chisel received different conservation treatment from the others; it is this which accounts for the variation in colour

Weighing equipment has been a standard tool for merchants and traders since Roman times, and illustrated here are some fine Viking-Age and medieval examples.

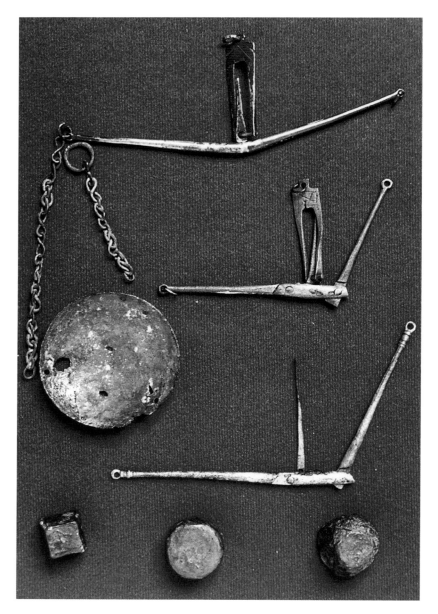

Tenth-century copper alloy balances (length of top balance 126mm). The upper one has fixed arms and still has one of its pans and attaching chains. The other two have folding arms. Three lead weights are at the bottom

Two types of Viking-Age hand-held beam balances were found in Coppergate, with either rigid or folding arms. When assembled, a bronze pan would have hung on three chains from each arm of the scale. Both folding and non-folding balance types seem to have been used. The small size suggests that they were used for measuring out commodities such as coins, ingots, other precious metals or spices.

Weights would have been set in the pans of scales, and a small selection of lead weights would have been carried by the trader. Viking-Age weights of copper alloy, lead alloy, and lead or iron coated with non-ferrous metals have been found in York. Many attempts have been made to correlate archaeologically recovered weights with possible Anglo-Saxon, Scandinavian or medieval units of measurement, but without success.

The Viking-Age iron weight illustrated, coated in brass, is one of a pair and weighs approximately 22g. It is decorated with a stamped 'triskele' motif of linked curves with three dots within a circle of stamped dots and was probably imported from Scandinavia.

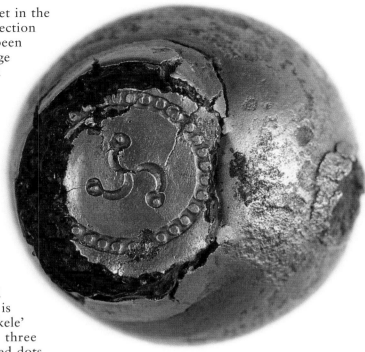

Viking-Age iron weight coated in brass (diameter 19mm)

The small Viking-Age lead weight with enamel decoration (11.8g) was excavated in 1976 on the site of the Clementhorpe nunnery. It is only some 15mm wide by 5mm deep but is highly unusual as the top is made of a reused earlier 8th-century enamel which has been cut down and set into the weight. A winged creature faces left and looks upwards, with a large head and an open mouth. The neck is short, and there is a narrow wing. The animal's leg is long and the foot enlarged.

Lead weight with enamel decoration (length 17mm)

Continued overleaf

Lead alloy pendant or weight in the shape of an anchor or ship (length 55mm)

The anchor-shaped or ship-shaped object illustrated may be a weight or a pendant. The upper end has a perforation which was presumably for suspension. Its weight of 26.37g is extremely close to the basic unit of weight of 26.6g identified amongst 200 Viking-Age weights from Dublin. It is certainly attractive enough to have been a pendant at some point.

The final shield-shaped weight illustrated here, from Coffee Yard, is much heavier at 227g, and comes from a different type of weighing system. This involved a steelyard which has un-equal arms, the long measuring arm having a weight suspended from it, which can be moved along the arm until equilibrium is obtained with the load suspended from the short arm. This lead alloy steelyard weight was cast in one piece and has a hole in the back for hanging onto a steelyard beam. It bears the royal coat of arms of Edward I, and is dated c.1290–1300.

Steelyard weight, late 13th to early 14th century (length 53mm)

Knife handle

Decorative handles for knives and other tools are not particularly unusual finds on medieval excavations in York. They are usually made of wood or bone, and may be socketed or formed from a pair of riveted plates; they often have simple line or dot decorations. Although knife handles are essentially functional objects, some examples are more elaborately decorated.

This knife handle was found on a site excavated in the 1990s near St Andrewgate. A quaint figure decorates a socketed bone handle which probably belonged originally to a knife. It appears very worn and well used and takes the form of a human of uncertain gender. It has a recognisable head with face and hair, but no obvious limbs, although lightly cut lines running most of the length of the body may represent folds in a long dress or cloak.

Much more deeply cut are the facial features, with small dots for eyes, a crudely cut nose and curious smiling mouth, pronounced chin, and flowing hair to each side. Across the forehead is a decorative headband.

Similar examples have been found elsewhere in England. Some feature more clearly female figures with a headband holding a headdress in place with buttons at the top of a gown or cloak. Others are also apparently armless with a veil and headdress, and with a hood depicted on the back. The simple nature of these figures probably reflects the difficulties involved in cutting shapes into bone, a material which much more readily lends itself to incised straight lines or stamped circles. Despite this, well-crafted aristocratic male and female figures, sometimes carrying hawks or small dogs, have been noted on a number of handles from other sites in England, north-western Europe and Scandinavia, all of much finer workmanship than the York example.

The York handle probably dates from around the 14th century. The fact that it is so worn may suggest it was lovingly kept and used for many years before reaching its final resting place.

Bone knife handle from St Andrewgate in the form of a human (length 84mm)

123

Hone stones

Hones or sharpening stones are widely distributed over archaeological sites, with over 200 found in Viking-Age levels in Coppergate alone. Many of the stones for these were imported from Norway, although archaeologist Richard Hall has suggested that such stone items may have been looked upon as saleable ballast for ships bearing more profitable goods such as exotic animal skins.

Viking-Age hone stones, some complete and some part-made

Hones or sharpening stones played an important role in the final stages of the production of iron blades, and also in the continuing maintenance of a sharp edge. Hones tend to be made of sandstone, schist or phyllite, and analysis of the stone indicates their place of origin. They frequently have worn grooves which probably resulted from sharpening. It is possible that the coarser-grained local sandstone may have been used for the initial sharpening, with the final honing done with finer-grained hones such as these of imported schist and phyllite. They come in a wide variety of shapes and sizes, ranging from small personal hones, which would have been perforated and suspended from a belt by a thong, to larger less portable examples.

Hones may have been traded as finished or part-made objects, or as raw material. There is evidence that hones were sawn to shape and sometimes perforated in York, as a number of unfinished hone stones have been excavated. The technique of making the hones involved splitting the stone, presumably with some sort of wedge or hammer, and then sawing the piece to the required size. There are many examples of hones which had been sawn halfway through and then crudely broken, leaving a rough end. The ends and surfaces could then be smoothed and used.

The number of hones found in and around certain wattle buildings in Viking Coppergate suggests that they may have been produced or finished off there, or used for local metalworking. For all we know, one of these hone stones may have been used to sharpen one of the objects featured in this book!

Medieval hone stone (sandstone) with a very pronounced groove (length 86mm)

Bow saw

This unusual bone object looks a bit like a Viking boomerang! It was originally interpreted as a piece of horse equipment (a horse-collar or saddlebow), but has now been reinterpreted by archaeologist Richard Hall as a handle or bow for a small saw.

It was excavated from Coppergate, and is late 9th or early 10th century in date. It is made of antler which has been shaped into a shallow curve. The thicker butt end has been cut obliquely, and the round end (the tip) has been sawn along two planes at approximately 90° to the lengthwise axis, and also along the inner arc of the curve. Towards the centre a rectangular slot transects the object. Within this slot, part of an antler peg has been retained. The object's surface is decorated with ring-and-dot motifs as well as incised crosses and chevrons.

A hypothetical reconstruction of this bow saw is illustrated here. It is thought that the blade would have been slotted into a cleft at the tip of the saw, and would then have been attached by a rivet to the plug, part of which survives within the rectangular slot. The tip end is roughly fashioned in comparison with the rest of the object, with two of the ring-and-dot motifs sliced away by knife or axe cuts. This may indicate subsequent refashioning or repair. It has been suggested that the cut at the tip end may have been for a spacer for a double saw, used for cutting comb teeth, to keep the blades apart.

No other bow saw like this one has been found in Anglo-Saxon England, although there is a representation of a large one in use on a 10th-century stone cross at Winwick in Cheshire. A figure, possibly the prophet Isaiah, is being held upside down and sawn in half by two assailants using a large bow saw. Hopefully the Coppergate example was used to fashion combs or similar objects!

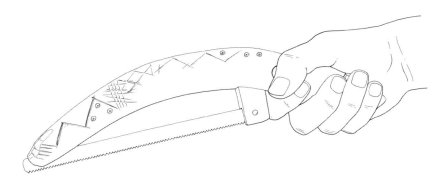

Reconstruction of the handle with its blade

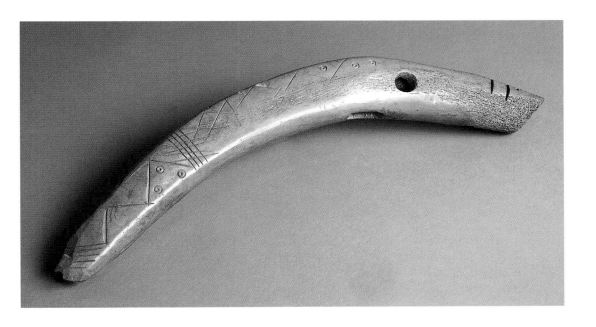

The front and back of the bow saw from Coppergate (length 288mm)

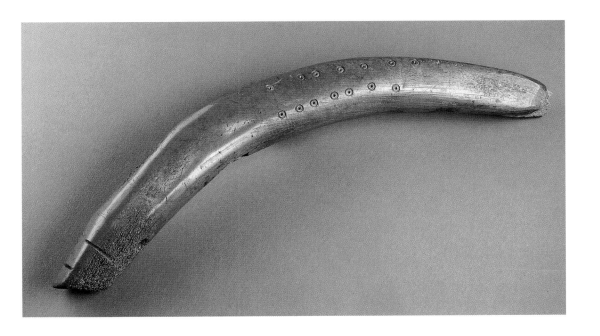

Beaver remains are uncommon, and these specimens from the 8th or 9th century are the first to be found in York. At the end of the last Ice Age the European beaver was distributed throughout most of Europe and northern Asia, from Scotland to eastern Siberia, but by the 8th century it seems that the beaver population was in decline over much of Britain due to hunting and the destruction of its woodland habitat.

These bones may have belonged to one animal that was probably taken for its fur and meat. Since several parts of the skeleton were found (including a lower incisor, part of a shoulderblade and a thigh bone), it was probably hunted locally rather than traded from a distance as pelt. Environmental archaeologist Terry O'Connor writes that there is evidence that beavers lived in the York area until at least the 8th century. Beavers are known for their construction of complex dams and underwater lodges, and it seems that substantial areas of wet woodland persisted at that time. In fact, the nearby pre-Norman Conquest place name Beverley is thought to be partly derived from the Old English *beofor* meaning beaver. The animals gradually became marginalised to the wilder parts of the country, and by the 10th century seem to have been scarce even in Wales. The Welsh king Hywel Dda valued a beaver at 120 pence, compared with a marten

Beaver (photograph by Sharon T. Brown, www.BeaversWW.org)

at 24 pence and a wolf at only 8 pence. One of the last accounts of the native beaver, again from Wales, was written by Geraldus Barri in 1190.

Beavers would have been used for food and fur, the latter prized for its beauty, warmth and waterproof qualities. They may even have been thought to have mystical qualities as beaver teeth are occasionally found as amulets in graves. The beaver was also the source of a valuable musk or drug known from classical times as *castoreum* which is naturally rich in a chemical similar to aspirin.

Strangely, it is beaver-chewed wood that is the commonest archaeological evidence of the beaver's existence, and several sites in Yorkshire, such as Skipsea and Starr Carr, have produced examples. Some of these pieces have been studied in York Archaeological Trust's conservation laboratories. Jim Spriggs, head of the conservation laboratories, has noted how well the individual incisor marks of the beaver are preserved, as well as spiral marks along the length of the wood where the bark has been stripped to expose the cambium (the beaver's main food source).

Since the 1920s, beavers have been reintroduced in a number of European countries, and by the early 1990s beaver numbers in Europe were estimated to have recovered to about 250,000. Their reappearance in Yorkshire, however, seems unlikely, and these few bones from York remain a significant find.

Above: Beaver bones found in an 8th-century ditch at Fishergate (maximum length 99mm)

Below: Beaver lower incisor found in a 9th-century ditch at Fishergate

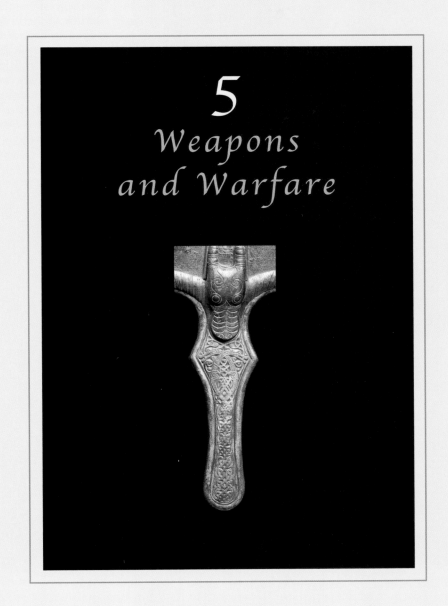

5
Weapons
and Warfare

How did the helmet end up buried in a pit? It was already quite old when it was buried: the brass decoration was worn from polishing and there were marks suggesting it had been worn and damaged in battle. Nevertheless such a fine possession would have remained a treasured heirloom. It had not been thrown casually in the pit; the mail and one cheek piece had been carefully placed inside. It might have been hidden to be retrieved later or perhaps it had been stolen and hidden by a thief. We can only imagine the circumstances in these turbulent times in York over a thousand years ago which led to the loss of this once-prized symbol of the valour, prowess and power of an Anglo-Saxon warrior.

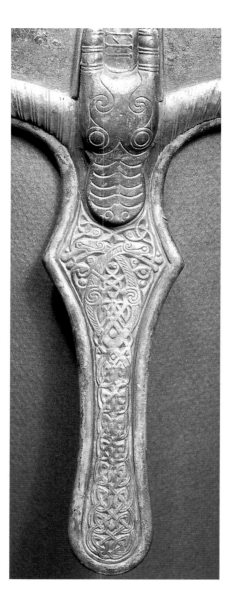

Above left: Detail of the name OSHERE on one of the brass strips

Above right: Detail of the animal and interlace decoration on the nasal

Detail of the animal head at the end of one of the eyebrows

Seax sheaths

Of all the thousands of objects recovered from Viking-Age Coppergate, very few were likely to have belonged to a warrior. Apart from a spearhead and a few fragments of sword, the only other iron weapon identified was a seax, a type of knife with a one-edged blade, which looked like a large version of a domestic knife but was used exclusively as a weapon. These knives have been found in pagan Saxon graves of men, often accompanied by other weapons such as spears and shields.

Although only one knife found at Coppergate was identified as a seax, several sheaths from the site are thought to have been made for this type of knife. These sheaths are made of calf leather, and have been formed by folding the leather into shape, the seam being where the cutting edge of the seax blade would have sat. A moulded ridge runs along the fold to add strength. The seam was closed with a series of metal rivets and/or stitching. It is clear from the position of the rivets on the first sheath that it would have been carried horizontally, but the method of suspension used on the second is not clear. Elaborate decoration was not found on all seax sheaths of this period, but both the Coppergate sheaths shown here were highly decorated. Each has large areas of interlace on one face, simpler cross-hatching on the other and key patterns along their seams; this pattern is repeated on the spine (or top edge) of the second sheath. Usually the decoration was applied by tooling, which was done by drawing a blunt-ended tool across wet leather, which left a permanent darker mark upon the leather when dry.

The lengths of the sheaths indicate the sizes of the knives they would have housed. They would, indeed, have been large, with blades approximately 170–200mm long.

Above left: Seax sheath with interlace and chevron decoration (length 330mm)

Above right: Seax sheath with interlace and key-pattern decoration (length 317mm)

Representation of a seax sheath, carried horizontally, on a 10th-century carved stone cross at Middleton church, North Yorkshire

The Vikings had a fearsome reputation as warriors, but evidence of such warlike types in Anglo-Scandinavian York is almost completely lacking. A few sword fragments and an occasional spearhead are all that have been recovered in recent years. Many residents of Jorvik would no doubt have owned swords, but these were probably prized possessions passed down the family and rarely thrown away. Nevertheless, at Coppergate, parts of four iron pommels, three pommel guards and three blade offcuts were found, all of which appeared to have been discarded during recycling for scrap, as all came from areas associated with metalworking.

Whalebone sword pommel from Coppergate (length 71mm)

An unusual piece of a Viking-Age sword is a five-lobed pommel, probably dating to the 9th or 10th century, and made of whalebone. This was also found at Coppergate, and was one of only two objects made from whalebone found on the site. It is not certain that the pommel was made locally. If it was, the bone may have been collected from a whale stranded on the east coast of Yorkshire, although there is also some documentary evidence of whaling in pre-Conquest England, recorded in Ælfric's *Colloquy*. Ælfric was abbot first at Cerne Abbas in Dorset and then at Eynsham in Oxfordshire, and he lived c.955–1010. His *Colloquy* was written as a dialogue for young monks and novices to practise Latin, which they had to learn to take part in the life of the abbey. In one section, a fisherman discusses with another the dangers of hunting whales: 'It is a risky business catching a whale. It's safer for me to go on the river with my boat, than to go hunting whales with many boats'. This suggests that whaling was undertaken from this country, these giant mammals presumably being hunted for their meat, as well as other useful products such as bone, fat and oil.

Other bone grips from swords are known, including an early 8th-century pommel guard from Fishergate, but their use may be more to do with appearance than with function. The

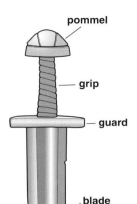

pommel

grip

guard

blade

main purpose of the pommel is to serve as a counterbalance to the iron blade, and bone would have been too light for this. Without pommels, all of the weight was beyond the grip, making the sword rather clumsy to use, much like an axe. It seems likely that bone pommels and grips were used on swords designed for appearance rather than as functional weapons.

Left: Diagram to show the component parts of a sword

Above: Iron sword pommel (left) and hilt guard (right) from Fishergate (length of pommel 50mm, guard 70mm)

Below: Bone pommel guard from Fishergate (length 72mm)

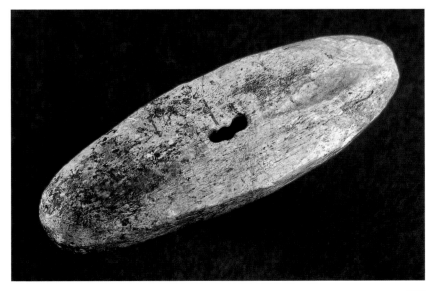

Enamelled belt fitting

In the Roman period, just as today, soldiers wore uniforms. In the early 2nd century, for example, all soldiers wore military tunics. These were much like those worn by ordinary Roman citizens, but were distinctively shorter, identifying the wearer as a military man. The concept of uniform implies that everyone looks the same, but personal equipment such as belts and their fittings does not appear to have been standard, as this beautiful copper alloy object indicates.

Enamelled belt fitting (length 56mm)

It is a military belt plate dating to the first half of the 2nd century. It has been cast into shape with its concave sides and two heavy studs on the reverse for attachment, and then decorated. The decoration is formed by millefiori enamel inlaid in three panels. The two outer panels are white and set with flowers which appear black. The central panel consists of an outer ring of blue enamel with a white flower pattern, and an inner disc set with panels of blue and white chequerboard in a blue frame alternating with a larger blue and white chequerboard in a red frame. Millefiori is an Italian word meaning '1000 flowers'. This decorative technique involves the fusing of coloured strips of glass into a rod which can be drawn out to reduce its diameter and from which slices can be cut; these reveal the fused colours of the rod on their sliced surfaces.

It may seem surprising that decorated as well as plain belt plates are well known from military sites, but soldiers were well-paid and privileged members of Roman society, who probably spent little time actually wearing armour or carrying shields and weapons. One way for a soldier to advertise his status would be by carrying a sword suspended from his belt — lavishly decorated belt fittings would have added to the overall impression of a man of importance in society. This particular example, which appears undamaged and may have been lost accidentally, was found during excavations within the fortress. It probably belonged to a soldier of the sixth legion, stationed at the fortress from about AD 120.

Cheek-piece from a Roman helmet

It is perhaps surprising that, despite several excavations within the area of the Roman fortress in York, very little in the way of military equipment has been found. One particularly interesting object, however, is this fragment of a helmet. It was found during excavations at the Purey Cust hospital, whose buildings stand just within the north-west defences of the Roman fortress, in a drain or ditch in an area which probably contained barrack blocks.

The helmet fragment comprises a damaged but virtually complete copper alloy cheek-piece from the left side of a helmet (as worn). A significant characteristic is the ear extension in the top right-hand corner. This indicates that the helmet would originally have belonged either to a cavalryman or, more likely, to one of the *equitates legionis*, horsemen who acted as escorts and messengers to the legion; the helmets worn by the infantry never incorporated such features. The cheek-piece would originally have had an iron backing because the thin copper alloy sheet would have offered little protection on its own, and it would have been hinged at the top. It has been decorated with embossed cabled borders which divide the cheek-piece into zones with a rosette on the large central area. There are faint impressions of the Roman numeral XII on the inside of the guard close to the rosette. These may be ghosts of marks impressed on the missing backing, and they may have functioned as identifying marks to distinguish the helmet of one soldier from another.

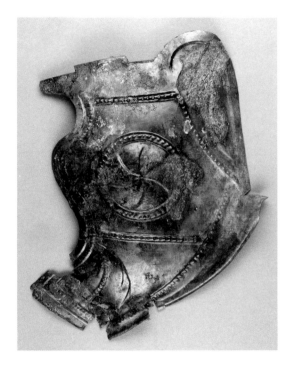

Copper alloy helmet cheek-piece (length 190mm)

Comparison with other helmets suggests that this one might date to the late 1st or early 2nd century AD, when the ninth legion was in York. Quite how this helmet fragment came to end its days in a drain in one corner of the fortress we can never know for certain. It may have been destined for repair or recycling by

the smiths who would have worked for the legion, making and repairing their armour and weapons. We can be sure, however, that the *equitates legionis,* mounted on their horses and with their finely decorated helmets, would have made a splendid sight on the streets of Roman York.

Reconstruction of a scene from the Roman fortress at York showing a soldier wearing the sort of helmet from which the cheek-piece came

In recent years we have all been encouraged to recycle more of our waste, but if we thought that reuse of materials was a modern phenomenon, we would be quite wrong. In fact, this small leather object is a fine example of medieval recycling. It is a bracer, which protected the inside of an archer's forearm against the snap of the string when shooting a longbow. It was found amongst a large quantity of waste leather — mainly offcuts from the manufacture and repair of shoes — in a late medieval layer at 16–22 Coppergate, and it has itself been made from reused shoe parts. A cut-down shoe sole forms the guard while the shoe straps and buckle are used for attaching the guard to the arm. The sole has come from a *poulaine* shoe, a style popular in the later 14th century, which featured elongated and pointed toes, sometimes extending up to 100mm beyond the tip of the big toe. Enough of the original shoe remains to show that this particular example was fastened with a buckle and loop over the instep.

Archery was considered an essential skill in the medieval period, and various laws were passed relating to the sport. The Statute of Winchester of 1285 required all men to own bows and arrows, to fit them for war. At the time of the Hundred Years War, however, the national skill at archery was deemed inadequate. In 1365 King Edward III complained that people preferred ball games and cockfighting which he considered dishonest and useless, and he ordered the entire male population to practise with bows and arrows or bolts on feast days (see p.78). A later law, the Statute of Cambridge, passed in 1388, reiterated Edward's demands, and insisted that all young men should give up recreations such as quoits, skittles and games of chance to do archery practice on Sundays and festivals. By the early 16th century, even boys as young as seven were expected to be provided with a bow and two arrows, and to be taught how to shoot, and every town had to set up butts or targets.

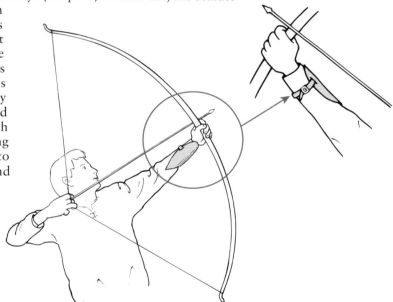

Diagram showing how an archer's bracer was used

Front and rear view of the archer's bracer made from reused shoe parts
(length of guard 127mm)

This piece of worked bone, found during excavations at the former St Leonard's Hospital site in 2003, looks at first glance rather unpromising. But it has aroused some excitement because it is, in fact, part of a bow, and thus a rare find of Roman military equipment.

Roman bows were composite: at the heart of the weapon was a wooden grip from which flexible arms sprang on either side. At each tip, a rigid 'ear' or angled end was cut. Each ear had a pair of laths or splints for reinforcement, one fixed to either side, with a notch cut out at one end to hold the ends of the bowstring. These laths would be made of bone or antler. Typically, they are elongated and curving blade-like strips, usually rounded and wider at one end, with a D-shaped section, and with their underside roughened to allow them to be glued to the ear of the bow. The notch for the string is cut into one edge close to the rounded end.

Roman soldier with a composite bow

The York object is an incomplete lath, possibly discarded as a result of breakage. The fortress would no doubt have had a workshop where weapons and armour would be repaired. In the legionary fortress at Caerleon, Gwent, for example, a collection of approximately 50 bone splints was found in what was interpreted as a 3rd-century armourer's workshop.

Soldiers were taught archery as part of their training, presumably as a useful skill to keep in reserve, but specialists (*sagittarii*) were also employed amongst the soldiers. These were usually auxiliaries, who were not Roman citizens but came from allied or subject states. They tended to have very light armour and no helmets, and were particularly effective in laying siege to enemy towns. Practice would clearly have formed an important part of training and maintaining their skills, and evidence of this was recovered at the fort of Vindolanda on Hadrian's Wall in the form of numerous ox skulls which had been used in target practice!

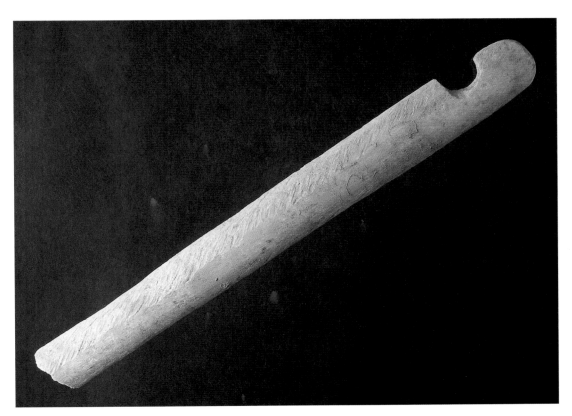

Fragment of a Roman bow found at the St Leonard's Hospital site (length 157mm)

6
Death and Ritual

Unguent bottle

In times past, when people often lived in an environment which was more insanitary than that of today, scents and perfumes were of great value in masking unpleasant odours. The Romans in particular were enthusiastic users of fragrances and scents — in the 1st century AD the city of Rome imported some 2,800 tons of frankincense and 550 tons of myrrh per year. Both men and women of wealth would literally bathe in perfume while attended by slaves. Taking this enthusiasm to extremes, Nero, Roman emperor in AD 54, spent the modern equivalent of £56,000 on scent for just one party he was giving!

Three types of perfume were applied to the body: solid unguents, scented oil and perfumed powders, all purchased from the shops of *unguentarii*, who were regarded every bit as highly as doctors. Small cosmetic bottles of the Roman period were called *unguentaria*, and today archaeologists come across them particularly when excavating Roman burials.

The complete unguent bottle here, which dates to the late 2nd or 3rd century, was found in an inhumation burial excavated in the Hungate area of the city in 2001. Unfortunately, all that remained of the skeleton were a few fragments of the skull, insufficient to identify the body as anything more than an adult of undetermined sex. So, what was the bottle doing there? One possible explanation is that it represented a treasured item belonging to the deceased. The best preserved and most complete Roman glass vessels have often been found in graves. Alternatively, the contents of the glass bottle, presumably an oil or perfume, may have been required in the burial rite, perhaps in the preparation of the body for the afterlife. We know of the use of perfumes in this way in the East at the beginning of the first millennium from a passage in the Bible:

While Jesus was in Bethany in the home of a man known as Simon the Leper, a woman came to him with an alabaster jar of very expensive perfume, which she poured on his head as he was reclining at the table. When the disciples saw this, they were indignant. 'Why this waste?' they asked. 'This perfume could have been sold at a high price and the money given to the poor.' Aware of this, Jesus said to them, 'Why are you bothering this woman? She has done a beautiful thing to me. The poor you will always have with you, but you will not always have me. When she poured this perfume on my body, she did it to prepare me for burial. I tell you the truth, wherever this gospel is preached throughout the world, what she has done will also be told, in memory of her' (Matthew 26: 6–13).

Glass unguent bottle dating from the late 2nd or 3rd century (length 99mm)

Oil lamp

This Roman ceramic oil lamp has travelled quite some distance in its life, because it was made in Gaul (Roman France) in around AD 70–140 but was found on the site of the Lion and Lamb public house on Blossom Street some 1900 years later. It may represent rubbish from the fortress or civilian settlement dumped on the site, which lay close to one of the main roads in and out of *Eboracum*. Perhaps it was discarded after its handle was broken off.

The lamp has been made using a two-part mould. Wet clay was pressed into each half of the mould and then the two halves were joined together. This was left to dry, before the moulds were removed and the two holes were pierced by hand. Finally, the lamp was fired in a kiln. Many lamps were decorated but this example is plain apart from the two lugs, one on each shoulder. There is a maker's mark in relief on the base, which indicates the specific workshop that created the lamp; unfortunately, in this instance, the maker's name is illegible.

A wick would have been inserted into the body of the lamp via the nozzle opposite the handle, and oil derived from plants would have been poured into the lamp through the filling hole on the top. The wick resting in the nozzle was lit and this produced a small flame. The flat base of the lamp meant that it could be set on any flat surface, and its small size ensured that it was easily portable. Although these lamps had a clearly functional role in everyday Roman life, they are also found in burials. They were believed to provide light on the journey to the underworld as well as serving as familiar objects from life to remind the dead of those left behind.

Small Roman ceramic lamp from Blossom Street (length 56mm)

Archaeological excavations are mostly carried out on site, but just occasionally they can occur in the laboratory. An almost complete soil-filled pot excavated from the Roman cemetery behind the Lion and Lamb public house in Blossom Street in 1989 provided conservator Martin Read with just such an opportunity.

Dalesware pot with chicken bones (diameter at rim 128mm)

The pot, identified as a Dalesware-type jar dating from the mid-2nd to the mid-3rd century AD, was found positioned above the skull of a burial. The conservator carried out the micro-excavation of the pot under a binocular microscope at x10 magnification.

Stones, charcoal and fragments of bone started to appear and all were plotted on a series of plans before removal. Gradually leg bones and a pelvis appeared, followed by ribs, wings, vertebrae, skull — and a wishbone! What we had was a chicken! The presence of a number of fragments identified as ossified ligaments indicated that it was an old chicken when it died. The position of the bones suggested that it had been lowered into the pot head first. The neck did not appear to join the head, but might have slumped after burial. The head was resting on a lump of dark earth tentatively identified as burnt turf or peat. Subsequent examination of the bones showed that the bird was male, and could thus have been a symbolic offering to the god Mercury, the 'Messenger of the Gods', to whom the cockerel was sacred.

Chicken bones, in fact, turn up quite frequently in Roman cemeteries. One of the skeletons uncovered by Channel 4's *Time Team* in the Roman cemetery under the lawn of the Royal York Hotel next to York railway station was of a young man who had chicken bones buried next to him, interpreted by the *Time Team* archaeologists as the remains of a 'feast for the dead' to mark his passage to the afterlife. Chicken bones have been found in several other Roman burial grounds in York, including the Roman cemetery at Trentholme Drive, close to the Blossom Street cemetery, where bird bones were found in five pots.

A pot such as this one, then, can tell us an extraordinary amount about life in the past. Not only can the bones, pot, earth and other contents be further analysed, but the practice of burial of such bones in cemeteries can be studied in its social, religious and historical context. Truly a complete excavation in miniature!

Relief sculpture from Rougier Street showing a cockerel, associated with the god Mercury (length 110mm)

Grave cover

Three fragments of 10th-century grave stones were recovered at Coppergate, but sadly none of them was found with a grave. One fragment appears to be part of a marker stone, while the other two, including the example illustrated here, are parts of grave covers. These would have been laid horizontally over the graves, perhaps in conjunction with a pair of upright end-stones. In fact, this particular stone appears never to have been used on a grave, but was discarded unfinished, and ended up being used as rubble. It is unclear how it found its way to Coppergate, but it may have come from either the church of All Saints, directly opposite the site on Pavement, or, perhaps more likely, from the church of St Mary Castlegate which backed onto the site. Excavations at St Mary's have produced 10th-century grave slabs and cross shaft fragments.

Limestone grave cover from Coppergate (length 230mm)

The grave cover is made of fine-grained Magnesian Limestone, and is possibly a piece of reused Roman building stone. The unfinished decoration on one face and the roughly prepared top both indicate that the piece was never completed. The decorative scheme on the more complete face comprises so-called 'ribbon beasts', with narrow ribbon-like extended bodies and clear animal features such as head and paws. These interlock, often in a confusing pattern. In this example, one of the two beasts is upside down. The other upright beast has a long neck tapering from his substantial chest which has a scroll immediately above the junction with the foreleg, which has a four-toed paw. The head has an incised elliptical eye and an unfinished nose, while the lower jaw hangs open and the ear extends into a band which binds both animals. The unfinished foot of the second beast lies in the mouth of the upright one. There is similar decoration on the other face. If the grave cover had been completed, it would probably have been painted. Similar images are found on many other carved stones of the period, and they appear almost to have been mass produced — the designs found on the Coppergate grave cover are so similar to those found on a cross-shaft fragment from the corner of Newgate/Patrick Pool, and also part of a grave cover from Clifford Street, that they may have been produced by the same craftsman.

Reconstruction of the complete design of two interlocked beasts on the grave cover

Colourful and decorative beads are not infrequent finds on archaeological sites in York (see p.62), but not all beads were made purely for adornment. Plain spherical beads of jet, amber or bone may once have belonged to rosaries, strings of beads usually assembled together with a cross, designed to help with the counting of prayers.

Often these rosaries would have been made up of beads of one material only, but they could contain beads of many materials. An inventory of the 14th-century King Charles V of France, for example, noted nineteen rosaries made of rose-tinted amber and coral with pearls for markers, as well as gold beads, jet beads with gold crosses, and black coral and pearls alternating with silver!

Group of amber rosary beads from Bedern and Fishergate (diameter of centre bead 8mm)

It is thought that rosaries were first used in England during the 11th century, and became increasingly popular from the 13th century. The craftsmen who made the beads and rosaries were known as *paternosters* (Our Fathers), named after the first prayer to be said with the rosary. During the medieval period, groups of artisans sharing a similar occupation began to form guilds. These associations acted for the mutual benefit of their members and soon began to prohibit the practice of their craft by non-members. The *paternosters* were one group who formed their own guilds. The York guild was set up in the 14th century. In London there is still a street named Paternoster Row in the area where these craftsmen worked.

Individual beads or pairs of jet and amber rosary beads have been recovered from a number of medieval ecclesiastical sites in the city, including the Gilbertine Priory of St Andrew, Fishergate, and the College of the Vicars Choral in Bedern. A more unusual find is a group of 66 jet beads, found all together on a site in North Street during excavations in 1993. They came from a single deposit dated to the late 13th/early 14th century, and included amongst them were at least two beads which appeared to be unfinished. Could these be the product of a *paternoster* on medieval North Street? The site is directly opposite All Saints' Church, which has been in existence since at least the late 12th century, so it would have been ideally placed for potential customers!

Group of jet rosary beads found in North Street

Gold and sapphire finger-ring

A magnificent gold finger-ring, set with a watery blue, hexagonal sapphire, was found on the site of the College of Vicars Choral at Bedern. It may have belonged to one of the vicars or to a visitor to the college. It seems to be in excellent condition and was lost, presumably accidentally, c.1350. Examination of the inside of the ring has shown that it was made in two parts, the head (or bezel) and the shoulders being one, and the remainder of the hoop the other. Compared with the pearl and garnet ring from Coppergate (see p.58-9), it is poorly made. The join between the shoulders and the hoop is clumsy on the inside, and the hoop itself is just a strip of gold. As a ring of some value, set with a comparatively rare stone — a natural blue sapphire, possibly from Sri Lanka — this lack of finish is surprising.

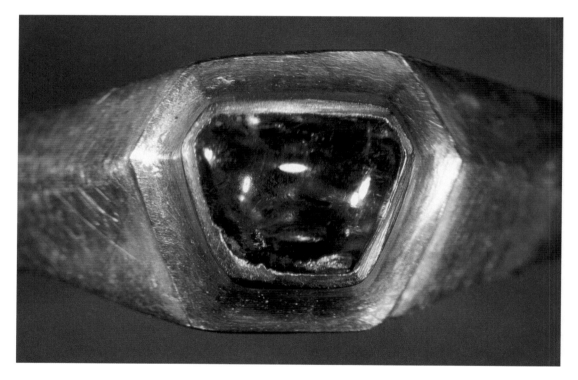

Detail of the sapphire setting in the gold finger-ring from Bedern (length of stone 5mm)

Sapphire rings appear to have been particularly associated with ecclesiastics, the blue colour symbolising the Virgin Mary's robe. At least a dozen such rings have been found in the graves of medieval bishops, some possibly representing the ring with which the bishop was consecrated. Elaborate 'pontifical' rings, worn by bishops when celebrating mass, have also frequently included sapphires, including that of the mid 13th-century Archbishop of York, Walter de Gray. His impressive ring, which was found in his grave, included not merely a fine and very large sapphire, but also four rubies and four emeralds. It is usually on display in the Treasury at York Minster. Bishops often had several pontifical rings. By the time of Edward I (1272–1307), the king had established his right to death duties on all bishops, which included a gold ring for himself, and the second best ring for the Archbishop of Canterbury!

Such valuable rings as this were clearly restricted to the few, but rings of base metals, such as copper and lead alloys, were made in far greater numbers than these grand examples, and often imitated their counterparts made of precious metals. Some used glass in their settings, often glass with a high lead content, to simulate gemstones, while rings of copper alloy were sometimes gilded to give the impression of gold.

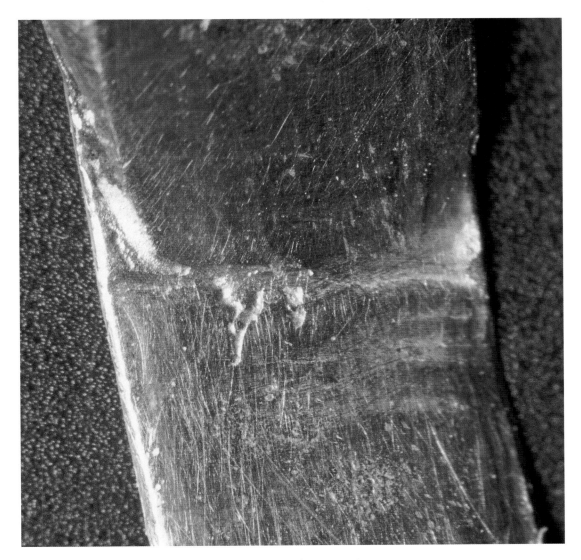

Detail of the inside of the ring showing the join between the two parts

Seal matrices, the stamps used to make seals in wax, are quite rare finds on medieval sites (see p.100-1). The seals themselves are not found, because wax does not survive an extended period of time underground. One form of seal which does, however, occasionally appear in archaeological deposits is a bulla, a lead alloy seal, which would have been attached to an official papal document sent out from Rome. Lead seals could only be used on papal documents, the seal acting to authenticate the document. As with other types of seal, the bulla would have been attached to the document by a silk ribbon.

Bullae were used by popes from the 6th century onwards, but the form of this bulla, found on the site of St Leonard's Hospital, was designed by Pope Pascal II, pope from 1099–1118, and it has been used unchanged up to modern times. On the front, and clearly visible, are the faces of St Peter (on the right as we look) and St Paul, separated by a cross. Peter is always represented with a crimped beard and curly hair, while Paul has short or no hair and a long beard. Above them are their abbreviated names: SPA(UL) and SPE(TER). On the reverse face the name of the issuing pope was written. In this case, much of the lettering has been worn away, but careful study and intensive conservation treatment has revealed enough detail to point to Pope Celestine III as the name most likely to be inscribed. Celestine was made pope in 1191 at the age of 85, dying seven years later.

There are a few doubts, however, as to the authenticity of this particular bulla. Inconsistencies in the shapes of the letters spelling out the pope's name have led one expert to suggest that this could be a forgery. But why would anyone forge a bulla? Medieval papal documents which have survived often relate to land, property or rents belonging to an ecclesiastical institution such as St Leonard's. Perhaps proof was required that a particular piece of land definitely belonged to the hospital, and perhaps the only way to provide that proof was by a forged papal document with its forged seal? Alternatively, perhaps the document belonged to an inmate of the hospital? We will probably never know.

Only two more examples of bullae have been found in excavations by York Archaeological Trust. Both came from excavations carried out on Peasholme Green, and both were found in graves, one clasped in the left hand of a skeleton. It has been suggested that bullae found in graves were most likely to have been originally attached to indulgences. These papal documents, which offered a pardon for a lifetime's sins, were often, ironically, corruptly bought from the Church!

Front and back of the papal bulla after having been cleaned at YAT's conservation laboratory (length 36mm)

This unusual flask-shaped object is made of tin, and was found during the Coppergate excavation, but what is it? In fact, it is an ampulla. Ampullae were made of tin or pewter, and were souvenirs designed for pilgrims to shrines in England and also in Europe. They were intended to hold holy oil or water that had been in contact with a saint. The earliest ones were made in Canterbury in 1171, within a year of St Thomas Becket's murder, and they represent some of the earliest examples of mass-produced goods. Ampullae were usually worn around the neck, suspended via the loops at the neck of the flask. As well as being proof of pilgrimage, they were also considered to be talismans and might be hung up in churches for the benefit of all in the locality. The Coppergate ampulla depicts the saintly figures of Peter and Paul, associated with York Minster from the 8th century onwards. It also appears to show an archbishop who may be identified as the 12th-century Archbishop William of York, subsequently canonised as St William.

Front and back of the tin ampulla from Coppergate (length 61mm)

St William was born William Fitzherbert. His father was the Chancellor and Treasurer of King Henry I, and his mother was half-sister of King Stephen and granddaughter of William I. He is recorded as Treasurer of the Cathedral of York in 1127, and then in 1141 he was elected Archbishop, only for his appointment to be quashed by the pope in 1148. Six years later, when he was reinstated, a famous incident occurred: on his return to York, he was escorted into the city by a huge crowd. As they crossed the wooden bridge over the River Ouse, the timbers gave way and large numbers of people were thrown in to the river. William prayed to God to spare them and, as he made the sign of the cross, all were saved. Three weeks later, William himself died, allegedly by poison in the chalice at mass. Within a few months of his death, he was said to be responsible for miracles, and then in 1223 sweet-smelling oil flowed from his tomb; this was a phenomenon thought to indicate sanctity. So, on 8 June 1227, on the 73rd anniversary of his death, he was proclaimed a saint by the pope. Eventually, in 1284, in a splendid ceremony involving King Edward I, his queen and numerous bishops and barons, William's remains were moved to a new shrine behind the high altar. His relics were placed in reliquaries and carried round the city in solemn procession on the anniversary of his death, and his tomb was always decked with gifts from those who had successfully invoked his help. William's coffin can still be seen in the crypt of York Minster.

Despite all these efforts, the cult status of St William, almost certainly seen as a northern rival to St Thomas of Canterbury, never seems to have equalled that of his hugely successful southern counterpart. While many ampullae and pilgrim badges associated with St Thomas have been recovered, only two St William ampullae from Coppergate seem to have survived, even though such objects would surely have been made in large numbers in York during the years following his canonisation.

Detail from the St William Window in York Minster, showing the collapse of Ouse Bridge in 1154 (reproduced by kind permission of the Dean and Chapter of York: © Dean and Chapter of York)

Chalice and paten

Objects placed in burials often provide very useful information about the person with whom they were buried. In the case of these objects — part of a pewter chalice and a paten — even if the body had been absent, we would still know that the person must have been male and a priest. In fact, the body was well preserved and easily identifiable as an adult male, 40–50 years old. He was found in a 13th-century cemetery attached to the Gilbertine Priory of St Andrew, Fishergate.

The pewter chalice and paten are copies of the silver vessels used to celebrate Holy Communion. In the ceremony, the chalice contained the wine, and the paten, or plate, held the wafer or bread. These copies were designed not for use in communion, but to accompany the burials of priests. William of Blois, Bishop of Worcester, ordained in 1229 that every church should have two chalices, one of silver for celebrating mass, and another of pewter which was unconsecrated and might be buried with the priest.

Pewter chalice and paten from Fishergate (diameter of paten 112mm)

The bowl of the chalice has lost fragments of the rim, but it is otherwise almost complete. The stem is broken below the single beaded knop as it begins to flare out, and fragments of the foot survive separately. The paten is complete apart from two fragments broken off the beaded rim, and it is slightly dished.

They were found lying over the stomach of the buried body, the arms of which may have been placed to hold the items. The chalice was in an upright position, but the original position of the paten is unclear; it was probably placed so that it covered the bowl of the chalice, which may have contained wine. Although not visible on this paten, in other examples found by archaeologists, traces of textile impressions on the undersides indicate the possible use of cloths over the chalice and under the paten in the burial ritual.

Chalice and paten (centre) as found with the burial (scale unit 0.1m)

Neolithic axe

A very unusual find for York is this splendid large, pale cream-coloured limestone axe. It is unusual because prehistoric finds in the city are quite rare. This particular object pre-dates the arrival of the Romans in York by some 3,000–4,000 years! The rough surface has shallow grooves in the two flat surfaces and at the edges — these appear to be natural strata which have eroded more than the surrounding layers. There are also grooves running at 45° to the bands, which may be evidence of wear from binding the axe to a handle.

The axe was recovered in 1999 on Watson Street, off Holgate Road, a site immediately west of York railway station. A hoard of 35 Neolithic flint tools was found in the same vicinity, near Holgate Beck, in 1868. This included seven axes with sharp edges, which could have been for cutting wood, although they do not seem to have been actually used. The more recently discovered axe was found with sherds of late Neolithic pottery, again rare finds for York, and also some pebbles, which appeared to have been subjected to heat and may therefore have been pot-boilers — hot stones thrown into water to keep it boiling during cooking. This axe is made of a local stone and was probably too soft to have been used as a tool. It is more likely to have had a ritual function. More research in the area where the axe was found may enable us to determine whether the site was used for occupation or perhaps for the making of ritual offerings.

Neolithic axe found in York (length 266mm)

Christ Child stained glass

When the site of St Andrew's Gilbertine Priory in Fishergate was excavated in the mid-1980s, considerable evidence was recovered of the devastation suffered by the buildings when the priory was dissolved during Henry VIII's Reformation of 1538–40. Piles of window glass were found together on floors, the lead framing or 'cames' having been systematically removed from the windows for melting down. Approximately 50,000 fragments of glass were recovered in total, some with exquisite decoration.

One of the most charming pieces is made up of three fragments of clear glass which fitted together to show the figure of the Christ Child cradled in elegant hands, no doubt those of the Blessed Virgin Mary. She appears to be giving the Christ Child a round object, such as a piece of fruit; other interpretations suggest the object represents her breast for Him to suckle from. The style of painting, especially the head and drapery of the Child, suggest a date in the 1320s or 1330s, when both documentary and archaeological evidence show that a major programme of rebuilding and alteration took place at the priory, including the rebuilding of the chapter house. This fragment was recovered from the chapter house and may have adorned one of its windows for almost 200 years, until the building was destroyed. It was then buried for another 450 years before being discovered by archaeologists.

1cm

Figure of the Christ Child on window glass from St Andrew's Priory, Fishergate (area of glass 31 cm²)

Stained glass windows in churches were not intended to be mere decoration. They helped to provide an atmosphere of reverence and worship in a sacred place. More importantly, they provided a visual aid, teaching the Gospel in an age when few people could read. The glass found at St Andrew's was probably made in York, where a number of master glaziers ran workshops during the medieval period, many living in the Stonegate area. To this day, St Helen's church just off Stonegate bears the arms of the medieval guild of York glass-painters in one of its windows.

York Minster is one of the great icons of medieval York. It has dominated the city for over 700 years, during which time stonemasons have been working almost non-stop to build, elaborate, repair and conserve this ancient structure. As fashions changed and new decorative schemes were developed, carved stone was removed and sometimes reused. Even today walls and gardens around the Minster are littered with fragments of carved stone whose source is probably the Minster. In the medieval period, as today, the Minster had its own stone workshops, and one possible product from these workshops, discarded unfinished, is illustrated here.

This small broken figure sculpture is made of Magnesian Limestone. It was intended to be freestanding but it was never finished and is badly damaged. The head has been roughly removed at the neck, and the arms have also broken off. The figure is female, kneeling on a small animal-like creature. Her right arm appears to have originally extended forward, perhaps to grasp something, while her other arm hung free. She is dressed in a tabard-like surcoat with circular neckline, and a tunic beneath. The small animal-like figure on which she kneels is unfinished, but it is possible to see one hind leg and one foreleg, and the head looking upwards and backwards in an impossible position. The face has a long thick nose, eyes, a brow and two long ears.

We are able to tell from the tool marks left on the sculpture how it was produced. First the block was roughly shaped using a fine-toothed blade, then the surface shape and some of the detail was blocked out using a narrow mason's point. Finally the surface details were smoothed out using a combination of the same mason's point and some form of abrasive, probably sandstone.

So, who was this figure? There are several possibilities: a female saint, a patron of the church or, most likely, a depiction of a Virtue conquering a Vice. This was a favourite scene in medieval England

Front view of the unfinished statue from Bedern (height 218mm)

and there are good examples elsewhere in the country which show Virtues in similar postures 'subduing' Vices, depicted as strange subhuman figures. Which Virtue might she represent? A good suggestion is Joy overcoming Idleness, and this is how the figure has been reconstructed here. Figures such as these would originally have been painted, and colours can be reconstructed from traces which survive on other sculptures.

Despite the unfinished nature of the drapery, the figure can be dated by her costume to around 1300. Although found in a pit at the College of Vicars Choral at Bedern, it is unlikely that she was destined to adorn the college. She probably represents an unfinished piece from the workshop of a school of sculptors who had recently completed the sculptural decoration of the Minster chapter house and she may have arrived at the college for use as rubble. Archaeological investigation rescued her from an ignominious end, and she can now be seen in all her glory.

Above: Hypothetical reconstruction of the intended appearance of the York sculpted figure as a Virtue overcoming a Vice

Right: Statue of a Virtue overcoming a Vice from the archway into the chapter house at Salisbury Cathedral

Further information about the objects

Publications cited:

AY: *The Archaeology of York* series; AYW: *The Archaeology of York on the web* series

2000 Years of York: the Archaeological Story (YAT, 1999)

Artefacts Alive! (2002) www.yorkarchaeology.co.uk/artefacts

AY 6/1, *Coney Street, Aldwark and Clementhorpe, Minor Sites, and Roman Roads* by David Brinklow, R.A. Hall, J.R. Magilton and Sara Donaghey (1986)

AY 7/2, *Anglian York: A Survey of the Evidence* by D. Tweddle, J. Moulden and E. Logan (1999)

AY 10/4, *The College of the Vicars Choral of York Minster at Bedern: Architectural Fragments* by David A. Stocker (1999)

AY 10/5, *The Vicars Choral of York Minster: The College at Bedern* by Julian D. Richards (2001)

AY 10/7, *Medieval Metalworking and Urban Life at St Andrewgate, York* by Rhona Finlayson (2004)

AY 11/3, *The Window Glass of the Order of St Gilbert of Sempringham: A York-based Study* by C. Pamela Graves (2000)

AY 14/4, *Environment and Living Conditions at Two Anglo-Scandinavian Sites* by A.R. Hall, H.K. Kenward, D. Williams and J.R.A. Greig (1983)

AY 15/4, *Bones from 46–54 Fishergate* by T.P. O'Connor (1991)

AY 16/5, *Anglo-Scandinavian Pottery from 16–22 Coppergate* by A.J. Mainman (1990)

AY 16/7, *Roman Pottery from the Fortress: 9 Blake Street* by Jason Monaghan (1993)

AY 16/8, *Roman Pottery from York* by Jason Monaghan (1997)

AY 17/3, *Anglo-Scandinavian Finds from Lloyds Bank, Pavement, and Other Sites* by Arthur MacGregor

AY 17/5, *Textiles, Cordage and Raw Fibre from 16–22 Coppergate* by Penelope Walton (1989)

AY 17/6, *Anglo-Scandinavian Ironwork from 16–22 Coppergate* by Patrick Ottaway (1992)

AY 17/8, *The Anglian Helmet from Coppergate* by Dominic Tweddle (1992)

AY 17/9, *Anglian and Other Finds from 46–54 Fishergate* by Nicola Rogers (1993)

AY 17/10, *Finds from the Fortress* by H.E.M. Cool, G. Lloyd-Morgan and A.D. Hooley (1995)

AY 17/11, *Textile Production at 16–22 Coppergate* by Penelope Walton Rogers (1997)

AY 17/12, *Craft, Industry and Everyday Life: Bone, Antler, Ivory and Horn from Anglo-Scandinavian and Medieval York* by A. MacGregor, A.J. Mainman and N.S.H. Rogers (1999)

AY 17/13, *Craft, Industry and Everyday Life: Wood and Woodworking in Anglo-Scandinavian and Medieval York* by Carole A. Morris (2000)

AY 17/14, *Craft, Industry and Everyday Life: Finds from Anglo-Scandinavian York* by A.J. Mainman and N.S.H. Rogers (2000)

AY 17/15, *Craft, Industry and Everyday Life: Finds from Medieval York* by Patrick Ottaway and Nicola Rogers (2002)

AY 17/16, *Craft, Industry and Everyday Life: Leather and Leatherworking in Anglo-Scandinavian and Medieval York* by Quita Mould, Ian Carlisle and Esther Cameron (2003)

AY 18/1, *Post-Roman Coins from York Excavations 1971–81* by E.J.E. Pirie (1986)

AYW 3, *Anglo-Scandinavian and Roman remains at 28–29 High Ousegate, York* by Neil Macnab and Jane McComish (2004) www.yorkarchaeology.co.uk/waterstones

Interim 1/3, 'The Seal of Snarrus' in *Archaeology in York: Interim*, volume 1, number 3 (1973)

Interim 8/4, 'Sugar and Spice' by Cathy Brooks in *Archaeology in York: Interim*, volume 8, number 4 (1982)

Interim 9/2, 'Sugar and Spice' by Cathy Brooks in *Archaeology in York: Interim*, volume 9, number 2 (1983)

Interim 14/2, 'Ceramic vessels with a horticultural use' by Sarah Jennings in *Archaeology in York: Interim*, volume 14, number 2 (1989)

Interim 14/4, 'Waxing lyrical' by Sonia O'Connor in *Archaeology in York: Interim*, volume 14, number 4 (1990)

Interim 15/3, 'The General Accident waxed tablets Part II: the lost word and other missing parts' by Sonia O'Connor in *Archaeology in York: Interim*, volume 15, number 3 (1990)

Interim 15/3, 'Coq au Vin, a Feast Fit for the Gods' by Martin Read in *Archaeology in York: Interim*, volume 15, number 3 (1990)

Interim 15/4, 'The General Accident waxed tablets Part III: open the box!' by Dominic Tweddle in *Archaeology in York: Interim*, volume 15, number 4 (1990)

Interim 20/4, 'Lost and Found' by Nicky Rogers in *Archaeology in York: Interim*, volume 20, number 4 (1995)

Interim 23/4, 'Bead-Gorrah! An Irish 'string' bead in Viking York' by Carole Morris in *Archaeology in York: Interim*, volume 23, number 4 (2001)

Yorkshire Archaeology Today No.2, 'From Roman fortress to air-raid shelter: the results of the St Leonard's Hospital excavation 2001' by Kurt Hunter-Mann (January 2002)

Yorkshire Archaeology Today No.5, 'A papal bulla from St Leonard's Hospital' by Nicky Rogers (July 2003)

All these publications are available from York Archaeological Trust.

For further information email: ckyriacou@yorkarchaeology.co.uk or see: www.yorkarchaeology.co.uk/pubs/pubs.php

Object	Page number	Site name	Site code	Small find number or accession code	Publication and YAT catalogue number	Location of object
Hearth and home						
Repaired wooden bowl	15	16–22 Coppergate	1976.7	7758	AY 17/13, 8542	JORVIK
Repaired wooden bowl	15	16–22 Coppergate	1976.7	375	AY 17/13, 8559	YAT
Head pot	16	Wellington Row	1987.24		AY 16/8, 3265	YAT
Head pot	17	24–30 Tanner Row	1983.32		AY 16/8, 1448	YAT
Female head pot	17	York cemetery, 1888		YORYM: H.2132	AY 16/8, 3246	Yorkshire Museum*
Male head pot	17	Priory Street, 19th century		YORYM: H.2135	AY 16/8, 3247	Yorkshire Museum*
Cage cup glass fragment	18	9 Blake Street	1975.6	800	AY 17/10, 5923	YAT
Blue glass fragment	18	Bedern	1978–9.14.II	227	AY 17/15, 13535	YAT
Glass bottle	19	St Leonard's Hospital	2001.10746	558		YAT
Bacchic cup	20	Wellington Row	1987.24		AY 16/8, 3148	YAT
Glass slick-stones	21	16–22 Coppergate	1976.7	7990, 13121, 8177	AY 17/11, 6592–4	JORVIK
Glass slick-stones	21	16–22 Coppergate	1976.7	3672, 3510, 3687	AY 17/11, 6595–7	YAT
Stone slick-stones	21	16–22 Coppergate	1976.7	10185, 11010	AY 17/11, 6579–80	YAT
Stone slick-stones	21	16–22 Coppergate	1976.7	11072	AY 17/11, 6581	JORVIK
Storage pitcher	22	16–22 Coppergate	1976.7		AY 16/5, 2141	JORVIK
Quern stones	23	46–54 Fishergate	1985.9	5271–2	AY 17/9, 4513	JORVIK
Box lid with bone mounts	24	16–22 Coppergate	1976.7	3572	AY 17/12 and 17/13, 6964	JORVIK
Needles	25	Bedern	1973.13	2008, 2384	AY 17/15, 14178–9	YAT
Needles	25	Bedern	1978–9.14	500, 414	AY 17/15, 14175, 14180	YAT
Needle	25	22 Piccadilly	1987.21	677	AY 17/15, 13030	YAT
Netting needle	26	Bedern	1973.13	679	AY 17/15, 14184	YAT
Netting needle	26	16–22 Coppergate	1976.7	2575	AY 17/11, 6634	YAT
Scissors	26	Bedern	1973.13	2483	AY 17/15, 13741	YAT
Thimble	27	46–54 Fishergate	1985.9	2248	AY 17/15, 15146	YAT
Ebor flagon	28	9 Blake Street	1975.6		AY 167, 2820	YAT
Samian cups	28	9 Blake Street	1975.6		AY 167, 2745, 2747, 2762	YAT
Crambeck pot counter	29	16–22 Coppergate	1976.7		AY 16/8, 3205	YAT
Crambeck ware with warrior	29	16–22 Coppergate	1976.7		AY 16/8, 3206	YAT
Wicker box lid	30	16–22 Coppergate	1976.7	778	AY 17/13, 8931	YAT
Bucket	31	16–22 Coppergate	1976.7	4176	AY 17/13, 8742	YAT
Stone mortar fragment	32	Bedern	1973.13	2856	AY 17/15, 13462	YAT
Stone mortar	33	16–22 Coppergate	1976.7	946	AY 17/15, 11031	YAT

Item	No.	Site	Accession	Find no.	Reference	Repository
Stone pestle	33	Bedern	1976.14	922	AY 17/15, 13473	YAT
Plant-holder	34	16–22 Coppergate	1976.7		Interim 14/2, pp.41–4; Medieval Archaeology 1984, p.194	YAT
Plant-holder	35	Bedern	1973.13		Interim 14/2, pp.41–4; Medieval Archaeology 1984, p.194	YAT
Keys	36	16–22 Coppergate	1976.7	5357, 6136, 6988	AY 17/6, 3665–6, 3673	YAT
Padlock	37	16–22 Coppergate	1976.7	11758	AY 17/6, 3610	YAT
Human waste	38	6–8 Pavement	1972.21		AY 14/4	JORVIK
Lavatory seat	39	16–22 Coppergate	1976.7	16280	AY 17/13, 8950	YAT
Mosaic	40-1	Clementhorpe Nunnery	1976.3		AY 6/1, pp.59–60	Yorkshire Museum
Mosaic	42-3	21–33 Aldwark	1973.5 YEG		AY 6/1, pp.40–41	Yorkshire Museum*
Mosaic	43	Old Malt Shovel Inn, Walmgate		YORYM: 1973.5		York Castle Museum

Dress, jewellery and personal possessions

Item	No.	Site	Accession	Find no.	Reference	Repository
Inscribed brooch	46	Merchant Adventurers' Hall	1995.1 YORMA	4	Interim 20/4, pp.34–5	Merchant Adventurers' Hall
Gold brooch	47	Bedern	1979.13.X	2847	AY 17/15, 14507	Yorkshire Museum
Strap-ends	48	46–54 Fishergate	1985.9	6264, 71	AY 17/9, 5320–1	YAT
Buckles	49	46–54 Fishergate	1985.9	1343, 3610	AY 17/9, 5311–12	YAT
Bone hair pins	50	9 Blake Street	1975.6	901, 929	AY 17/10, 6399–400	YAT
Jet hair pins	50	24–30 Tanner Row	1983.32	881, 894		YAT
Hair piece	50	Railway Excavations	1875	YORYM: 1998.695		Yorkshire Museum*
Jet hair pins	50	Railway Excavations	1875	YORYM: 1995.248/249		Yorkshire Museum*
Ringed pins	51	16–22 Coppergate	1976.7	13149, 13035	AY 17/14, 10478, 10480	JORVIK
Silk cap	52-3	16–22 Coppergate	1980.7	8129	AY 17/5, 1372	Yorkshire Museum*
Sock	54	16–22 Coppergate	1976.7	13517	AY 17/5, 1309	JORVIK
Leather shoes	55-6	16–22 Coppergate	1976.7	7663, 13711	AY 17/16, 15354, 15438	JORVIK
Shoe last	55	6–8 Pavement	1972.21	5021	AY 71/3, 494	Yorkshire Museum*
Amber pendants	57	16–22 Coppergate	1976.7		AY 17/14	JORVIK/YAT
Gold, pearl and garnet ring	58-9	16–22 Coppergate	1977.7	872	AY 17/15, 12937	Yorkshire Museum
Arm-rings	60	16–22 Coppergate	1976.7	7806, 8502	AY 17/14, 10499, 10608	JORVIK

Object	Page number	Site name	Site code	Small find number or accession code	Publication and YAT catalogue number	Location of object
Jet bracelet	61	24–30 Tanner Row	1983.32	830		YAT
Jet bracelet fragment	61	24–30 Tanner Row	1983.32	28		YAT
Emerald	62	46–54 Fishergate	1985.9	1121	AY 17/9, 4574	YAT
Glass bead	62	41–49 Walmgate	1999.941	4	Interim 23/4, pp.22–8	YAT
Chatelaine	63	46–54 Fishergate	1985.9	5054–5, 5057	AY 17/9, 5243–5	YAT
Prick spur	64	16–22 Coppergate	1976.7	8589	AY 17/6, 3826	JORVIK
Prick spur	65	16–22 Coppergate	1976.7	9955	AY 17/6, 3836	YAT
Inlaid knife	66	Bedern	1978.14.II	408	AY 17/15, 13777	YAT
Inlaid knife	67	Bedern Foundry	1973.13.II	542	AY 17/15, 13184	YAT
Inlaid knife	67	Bedern	1979.14.IV	5133	AY 17/15, 13792	YAT
Comb	69	16–22 Coppergate	1976.7	5704	AY 17/12, 7594	JORVIK
Comb	69	28–9 High Ousegate	YORYM 2002.457	34	AYW 3	YAT
Comb case	69	16–22 Coppergate	1976.7	12884	AY 17/12, 7690	JORVIK
Toilet implement	70	16–22 Coppergate	1976.7	2766	AY 17/15, 12923	YAT
Toilet set	70	46–54 Fishergate	1985.9	3057	AY 17/12, 8145	YAT
Tweezers	71	16–22 Coppergate	1976.7	6956	AY 17/14, 10531	JORVIK
Toothbrush	71	St Leonard's Hospital	2001.10746	520		YAT
Medical plate	73	46–54 Fishergate	1985.9	6025	AY 17/15, 15226	YAT
Games, recreation and literacy						
Bone skates	76-7	16–22 Coppergate	1976.7		AY 17/12	YAT/JORVIK
Bowling ball	78	16–22 Coppergate	1976.7	2665	AY 17/13, 9041	YAT
Gaming board	80	16–22 Coppergate	1976.7	6609	AY 17/13, 9032	JORVIK
Jet chess piece	80	1–2 Tower Street	1981.3	313		YAT
Walrus ivory gaming piece	81	16–22 Coppergate	1976.7	4949	AY 17/12, 7888	JORVIK
Bone die	82	46–54 Fishergate	1985.9	4264	AY 17/12, 8164	YAT
Jet dice	82	16–22 Coppergate	1976.7	3496, 4954	AY 17/15, 11078–9	YAT
Walrus ivory die	83	16–22 Coppergate	1976.7	6721	AY 17/12, 7890	JORVIK
Bone styli	84	Bedern	1976.13.X	2622, 1978, 2688, 2509	AY 17/12, 8037, 8039, 8040, 8053	YAT

	Page	Site	Accession	No.	Reference	Repository
Bone stylus	84	Bedern Foundry	1973–6.13	1459	AY 17/12, 7971	YAT
Bone stylus	84	2 Aldwark	1978–80.14	776	AY 17/12, 8122	YAT
Page holder	85	Bedern	1976.13.X	2776	AY 17/15, 14477	YAT
Lead slate	85	Bedern	1976.13.X	1992	AY 10/5	YAT
Wax tablets	86	12–18 Swinegate	1989.28	257	Interim 14/4, pp.36–9; Interim 15/3, pp.30–7; Interim 15/4, pp.25–34	YAT
Clay pipe	89	12 Minster Yard	YORYM 2003.305	1		YAT
Pan pipes	90-1	16–22 Coppergate	1976.7	5083	AY 17/13, 9038	JORVIK
Jew's harp	92	Bedern	1976.13.X	3380	AY 17/15, 14117	YAT
Tuning pegs	94	Bedern	1976.13.X	2342, 2877	AY 17/12, 8070–1	YAT
Tuning peg	94	Bedern	1979.14.IV	416	AY 17/12, 8065,	YAT
Tuning peg	94	2 Aldwark	1978–80.14	624	AY 17/12, 8124	YAT
Tuning key	95	16–22 Coppergate	1976.7	5734	AY 17/12, 7079	JORVIK
Buzz bone	96	16–22 Coppergate	1976.7		AY 17/12	YAT
Queen Victoria medallion	97	St Leonard's Hospital	2001.10746	253	Yorkshire Archaeology Today No.2, pp.2–3	YAT

Craft, trade and industry

	Page	Site	Accession	No.	Reference	Repository
Seal of Snarrus	100	21–33 Aldwark	1973.5 YEG	29	Interim 1/3, pp.37–8	Yorkshire Museum
Seal matrix	101	46–54 Fishergate	1985.9	3870	AY 17/15, 15241	YAT
Motif piece	102-3	16–22 Coppergate	1979.7	5692	AY 17/12, 6982	Yorkshire Museum*
Motif piece	103	16–22 Coppergate	1976.7	8016	AY 17/12, 6981	JORVIK
Wool comb	104-5	16–22 Coppergate	1980.7	10786	AY 17/6 and 17/11, 2273	Yorkshire Museum*
Flax rippler	105	16–22 Coppergate	1976.7	2805	AY 17/11, 6641	YAT
Tabby weave textile	107	16–22 Coppergate	1976.7	13326	AY 17/5, 1263	YAT
Silk	107	16–22 Coppergate	1976.7	8324	AY 17/5, 1347	YAT
Wool fibres	107	16–22 Coppergate	1976.7	416	AY 17/5, 1375	JORVIK
Wool yarn	107	16–22 Coppergate	1976.7	3258	AY 17/5, 1428	YAT
Wool textile	107	Coppergate watching brief	1982.22	247	AY 17/5, 1460	JORVIK
Coin dies	108, 110	16–22 Coppergate	1976.7	9351, 13993	AY 18/1, 43, 49	JORVIK
Trial piece	109–110	16–22 Coppergate	1976.7	4622	AY 18/1, 59	JORVIK
Samarkand coin	111	16–22 Coppergate	1976.7	10582	AY 18/1, 47	JORVIK

Object	Page number	Site name	Site code	Small find number or accession code	Publication and YAT catalogue number	Location of object
Sugar mould	113	Pawson's warehouse, Skeldergate	1983.25		*Interim* 8/4, pp.43–8; *Interim* 9/2, pp.28–30	YAT (sugar loaf in York Castle Museum)
Cat mandible	114	Bedern			AY 10/5	YAT
Red squirrel bones	114	Bedern			AY 10/5	YAT
Squirrel seal matrix	114	Bedern	1976–9.13.X	2805		YAT
Pine marten bone	115	46–54 Fishergate	1985.9		AY 17/15, 14484	YAT
Cowrie shell	116	16–22 Coppergate	1976.7	11163	AY 15/4	JORVIK
Flint 'thumb' scraper	117	St Leonard's Hospital	2001.10746	1635		YAT
Shears/clippers	117	Coppergate watching brief				JORVIK
Spoon bit	118	16–22 Coppergate	1982.22	229	AY 17/6, 2249	JORVIK
Draw-knife	118	16–22 Coppergate	1976.7	8542	AY 17/6, 2262	JORVIK
Chisel/slice	118	16–22 Coppergate	1976.7	7278	AY 17/6, 2259	JORVIK
Axe	118	16–22 Coppergate	1976.7	10108	AY 17/6, 2258	JORVIK
Wooden mallet	119	16–22 Coppergate	1976.7	7991	AY 17/6, 2253	JORVIK
Balances	120	16–22 Coppergate	1976.7	9604	AY 17/13, 8186	JORVIK
Weight	121	16–22 Coppergate	1976.7	7576, 9512	AY 17/14, 10405, 10409	JORVIK
Decorated weight	121	Clementhorpe Nunnery	1976.3	15879	AY 17/14, 10356	JORVIK
Weight	122	16–22 Coppergate	1976.7	4	AY 7/2, 81	Yorkshire Museum*
Steelyard weight	122	Coffee Yard	1991.18	7606	AY 17/14, 10583	Yorkshire Museum*
Knife handle	123	St Andrewgate	1995.89	59	AY 10/7	YAT
Hone stones	124	16–22 Coppergate	1976.7	505	AY 17/14 and 17/15	YAT
Hone stone with deep groove	125	46–54 Fishergate	1985.9		AY 17/15, 14745	YAT
Bow saw	127	16–22 Coppergate	1976.7	5112	AY 17/12, 7704	JORVIK
Beaver bones	129	46–54 Fishergate	1985.9	13165	AY 15/4	YAT

Weapons and warfare

Object	Page number	Site name	Site code	Small find number or accession code	Publication and YAT catalogue number	Location of object
Anglian helmet	132-5	Coppergate watching brief				York Castle Museum
Seax sheaths	136	16–22 Coppergate	1982.22	155	AY 17/8, 4418	JORVIK
Sword pommel (whalebone)	138	16–22 Coppergate	1976.7	8133, 13279	AY 17/16, 15659–60	Yorkshire Museum*
Sword hilt guard (iron)	139	46–54 Fishergate	1979.7	4752	AY 17/12, 6810	YAT
Sword pommel (iron)	139	46–54 Fishergate	1985.9	3953	AY 17/9, 5263	YAT
Sword pommel (iron)	139	46–54 Fishergate	1985.9	4459	AY 17/9, 5262	YAT

Item	No.	Site	Accession	Number	Reference	Location
Sword pommel guard (bone)	139	46–54 Fishergate	1985.9	8047	AY 17/9, 5612	YAT
Enamelled belt fitting	140	9 Blake Street	1975.6	96	AY 17/10, 6305	Yorkshire Museum*
Helmet cheek-piece	141	Purey Cust Hospital	1985.22	88	AY 17/10, 6528	YAT
Archer's bracer	143	16–22 Coppergate	1976.7	811	AY 17/16, 15748	YAT
Bow fragment	145	St Leonard's Hospital	2001.10746	3130		YAT
Death and ritual						
Unguent bottle	148	Dundas Street, Hungate	HUN02	116	AY 16/8, 3341	YAT
Oil lamp	149	35–41 Blossom Street	1989.21			YAT
Burial pot with chicken bones	150	35–41 Blossom Street	1989.21		AY 16/8, 3788; *Interim* 15/3	YAT
Cockerel sculpture	151	5 Rougier Street	1981.12	185		YAT
Grave cover	152	16–22 Coppergate	1977.7	2115	AY 17/14, 10826	Yorkshire Museum*
Amber rosary bead	154	Bedern	1976.13.X	2409	AY 17/15, 13506	YAT
Amber rosary bead	154	Bedern	1978.14.II	215	AY 17/15, 13507	YAT
Amber rosary bead	154	46–54 Fishergate	1985.9	7815	AY 17/15, 14775	YAT
Jet rosary beads	155	North Street	1993.1	33		YAT
Gold and sapphire ring	156–7	Bedern	1979.14.II	390	AY 17/15, 14508	Yorkshire Museum
Papal bulla	159	St Leonard's Hospital	2001.10746	2145	*Yorkshire Archaeology Today* No.5, p.5	
Ampulla	160	16–22 Coppergate	1977.7	2353	AY 17/15, 12966	YAT
Chalice and paten	162	46–54 Fishergate	1985.9	5712	AY 17/15, 15287	Yorkshire Museum
Neolithic axe	164	Watson Street	1999.251	2		YAT
Christ child stained glass	165	46–54 Fishergate	1985.9	3045	AY 11/3, 268	YAT
Unfinished sculpture	166	Bedern	1973.13	2834	AY 10/4, 286	YAT

* Yorkshire Museum = on display in the Museum as at April 2004

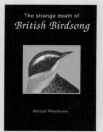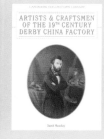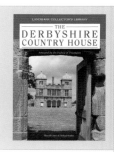

LANDMARK COLLECTOR'S LIBRARY

• The Strange Death of British Birdsong

Michael Waterhouse

ISBN: 1 84306 126 0. Full colour. Hardback. Price: £24.95.

• Historic Parks & Gardens of Cheshire

Linden Groves

ISBN: 1 84306 124 4. Full colour. Hardback. Price: £19.95.

• Colours of the Cut
The company colours of the inland waterway working boats of Britain

Edward Padget-Thomlinson

ISBN: 1 84306 145 7. Full colour. Hardback. Price: £24.95.

• Artists & Craftsmen of the 19th Century, Derby China Factory

David Manchip

ISBN: 1 84306 139 2. Full colour. Hardback. Price: £45.00.

• Old Crown Derby China Works, The King Street Factory 1849-1935

Robin Blackwood & Cherryl Head

ISBN: 1 84306 091. Hardback. Price: £49.95

• Derbyshire Country House

Maxwell Craven & Michael Stanley

ISBN: 1 84306 130 9. NEW complete paperback edition. Price: £24.95.

• Lost Houses of Derbyshire

Maxwell Craven & Michael Stanley

ISBN: 1 84306 064 7. Hardback. Price: £19.95.

Full details upon request.

Landmark Publishing Ltd
Ashbourne Hall, Cokayne Ave
Ashbourne, Derbyshire DE6 1EJ England
Tel: (01335) 347349 Fax: (01335) 347303
E-mail: landmark@clara.net Web site: www.landmarkpublishing.co.uk